NEW ENGLAND Sweets

Doughnuts, Bonbons & Whoopie Pies

SUSAN MARA BREGMAN

AMERICAN PALATE

Published by American Palate
A division of The History Press
An imprint of Arcadia Publishing
Charleston, SC
www.historypress.com

Front cover: Workers painting the Necco water tower in 1986. *Photo by Phil Barber*; Roll of Necco Wafers. *Courtesy of the Candy Wrapper Museum.*
Back cover: Whoopie pie and Sevigny's Ribbon Candy. *Courtesy of the author*; Vintage advertisement for Schrafft's chocolate bars. *Courtesy of David and Caroline Llewellyn.*

First published 2025

Manufactured in the United States

ISBN 9781467157483

Library of Congress Control Number: 2025935718

For everyone with a sweet tooth.

CONTENTS

ACKNOWLEDGEMENTS

A funny thing happened when I said I was writing a book about New England's sweets and treats: everyone wanted to join me on field trips.

So first, thank you to my road trip buddies. Nicki Rohloff rode shotgun as we tasted creemees and sampled maple syrup in Vermont, and she kept me calm when the Google navigatrix sent us down unpaved back roads or flat-out abandoned us in the rainy mountains. Maria and Joe Amador introduced me to Rhode Island's delicacies (although I drew the line at pizza strips) and graciously opened their home to me. Liz Budington joined me on confectionery adventures in Worcester, Salem, Somerville and Dorchester. And Dave Gallogly did not find it the least bit strange to drive an hour and a half just to try the best coffee cabinet in Rhode Island.

Patrick Myers invited me to be a judge at Maine's annual Whoopie Pie Festival, a bucket-list experience. Malaika and Gerard Picard gave me a tour of their Maine Needhams factory; Louise Mawhinney recounted her adventures as she brought Sky Bars back to life; and Jeff Green reminisced about his career at Necco.

I had the pleasure of connecting with Candy Daggett Young and her cousin Meredythe Schober, both of whom were part of the extended Daggett Chocolate family. I was delighted to hear firsthand stories about F.B. Washburn and the beloved Waleeco bar from Doug Gilson, about Deran Confectionery from Fred Hintlian and about the deliciously named Velvet Kisses from Eric Schultz. I talked about Marshmallow Fluff with author Mimi Graney and about Confectioner's Row with chocolatier Jeremy

Spindler. I learned a lot about ice cream from wide-ranging conversations with Judy Herrell and Gus Rancatore.

Thank you to the generous folks who shared photos, books and memorabilia from their collections: Jeff Green, Barb Froman, Eric Schultz, Candy Daggett Young, Meredythe Schober, Judy Herrell, Malaika and Gerard Picard, David and Caroline Llewellyn, Phil Barber and Judy Rosenberg. A special thank-you to Darlene and Joe Lacey. Darlene provided insights into the Necco universe and some welcome author-to-author advice. She and Joe generously provided extraordinary images from the Candy Wrapper Museum, and both connected me with other collectors of candy memorabilia.

Thank you to my friends and family for your suggestions, feedback and occasional pep talks, especially David Dao, Gloria Leipzig, Alisa Capaldi, Co Sarkis, Michael Bregman, Fern Drillings and Richard Bregman. (Rich, you were right about whoopie pies!) Thank you to Lainy Fersh for providing a key introduction. Thank you to Cindy Sragg (and Maggie) for taking such good care of my pup when I was traveling. Thank you to Sheila Powers and John Moore for an enjoyable conversation about sweets and treats on a June afternoon in Maine. I am truly grateful for the many healthcare professionals who got me back on my feet after total knee replacement surgery smack in the middle of my book schedule. And, finally, thank you to Mike Kinsella and the team at Arcadia Publishing for your expert advice and guidance.

Introduction

SWEET STUFF

In the beginning, I wanted to write a book about whoopie pies.

After all, these quintessential New England treats have a history with just enough intrigue to make a good story: interstate rivalry, competing festivals and a fight to become Maine's official treat. The story, like the pies themselves, was irresistible.

But after a few gentle suggestions to celebrate the wonderful whoopie but also explore the region's other confections—a legacy of candies, cookies, doughnuts, ice cream and more—I took the hint, and *New England Sweets* was born.

I tasted cider doughnuts, still hot from the fryer; molasses candy from an early nineteenth-century recipe; decadent chocolate from bean-to-bar manufacturers; and arguably the best coffee cabinet in Rhode Island. I took a deep dive into the confectionery history of Boston and Cambridge, where scores of candy makers created some of the chocolate bars we still eat today and others that are dearly missed. I spoke with descendants of the region's confectioners and visited candy factories in Connecticut, Maine and Massachusetts. I tried maple creemees in Vermont and doughboys in Rhode Island. And, yes, I was a judge at the 2024 Maine Whoopie Pie Festival and attended the nineteenth annual What the Fluff? festival in the pouring rain.

I combed through newspaper archives and pored over help-wanted ads to trace the rise and fall of Massachusetts candy makers. I delighted in fanciful and evocative names of their products, including elegant boxed chocolates branded as Romance and Luxuro and the penny candies and nickel bars called Nut Zipper, Waleeco and Mary Jane.

New England Sweets spans the region's history from the Native Americans who tapped maple trees and gathered wild blueberries to today's ice cream shops that dish out creamy portions of chocolate, vanilla and black raspberry.

The book tells a story of ingenuity, perseverance, scandal, tragedy, hard work, serendipity and a few sparks of genius. Potatoes in candy? Why not? What if we added cookie dough to ice cream or smooshed in some crumbled Heath bars? What should we call a sandwich that marries peanut butter and Marshmallow Fluff?

There is also a dark side to these otherwise sweet stories. Plentiful supplies of sugar and its byproduct molasses depended on the labor of enslaved workers on plantations, and child labor persists on some cacao plantations. Factories often burned down, and a molasses holding tank exploded in Boston to cause a devastating flood that killed twenty-one people and changed the city's streetscape.

But mostly, this is a happy story and often a nostalgic one. My friends reminisced about eating ribbon candy on Christmas Eve and buying Waleeco bars when they were kids. They recalled drinking coffee milk growing up and sharing the four flavors of Sky Bars with their friends. Ice cream fans remembered queuing up at the original Steve's Ice Cream in Somerville and patronizing the Brookline basement location of the first Emack & Bolio's. And arguing about the best cannoli in the North End is a popular Boston pastime.

New England Sweets presents an overview of the region's confectionery landscape and is organized as follows.

Chapter 1, "Starting from Scratch," sets the stage for the narrative with a brief history of the ingredients that form the building blocks of New England's confections: sugar, molasses and chocolate.

Chapter 2, "Food of the Gods," traces the history of chocolate from a bitter brew favored by the Mayans and Aztecs to the sweet creamy bonbons we enjoy today.

Chapter 3, "It Started with Necco," celebrates the enduring legacy of the New England Confectionery Company and the dozens of other candy makers in Boston and Cambridge from the nineteenth century to the present day.

Chapter 4, "Beyond Confectioner's Row," hits the road and focuses on the candy makers that settled in other parts of the region.

Chapter 5, "Fresh from the Oven," includes popular baked treats like brownies and Table Talk Pies.

Chapter 6, "Out of the Fryer," explores the stories behind favorites like doughnuts and cannoli.

New Englanders love ice cream no matter what the weather, and Chapter 7, "Frozen," traces the history of the region's best-known ice cream vendors.

Chapter 8, "Reinventing Ice Cream," pays homage to the pioneers who changed the way we think about ice cream.

Most states have named official foods, and Chapter 9, "Official Sweets and Runners-Up," wraps up the book by highlighting the sweets that made the cut in each of the six New England states (and a few wannabes).

The images in the book came from a wide range of sources, including the Library of Congress, Digital Commonwealth, New York Public Library, Penobscot Marine Museum, City of Boston, History Cambridge and private collections (including my own). I took the photographs marked "Courtesy of author." All images from the Candy Wrapper Museum are from the book *Necco—An Epic Candy Tale* by Darlene Lacey.

New England Sweets is a personal and affectionate look at the region's confectionery landscape. It is representative, not encyclopedic, and it is not meant to be a travel guide or a cookbook. While I sampled my fair share of sweets in the name of research, I could not visit every ice cream shop, doughnut seller, candy maker, chocolatier and bakery in New England. Nor was there room in this volume to include every place I visited. Instead, please consider this book a hint (an amuse-bouche, if you will) of the confectionery delights that await your next road trip.

Until then, I invite you to grab a whoopie pie, settle into your favorite spot and join me on a confectionery journey across New England.

Chapter 1

STARTING FROM SCRATCH

Sugar, Molasses and Chocolate

New England's love affair with sweets began early. In colonial times, Americans used molasses to sweeten favorites like Indian pudding and pumpkin pie, and they added sugar to the chocolate they drank both for pleasure and health. Boston's merchants traded in the essential raw ingredients—sugar, molasses and cacao—and the city was home to the country's first chocolate factory. It is no surprise that Boston became a confectionery capital.

SUGAR

American colonists used sugar as a sweetener, medicine and preservative, and Boston began importing sugar from Caribbean cane plantations in the late 1600s. The city's first sugar refinery came much later, when the Boston Sugar Refinery opened in 1834 on Lewis Street in East Boston. The factory was expanded in 1850 and soon was processing twenty-five million pounds of raw sugar a year.

Until the mid-1800s, sugar was distributed in solid blocks or cones; consumers would use a scissor-like tool called a "sugar nip" to cut off pieces small enough to sweeten their afternoon tea. The Boston Sugar Refinery was the first to develop granulated sugar and help send sugar nips on the road to obsolescence. In 1887, the company became part of the Sugar Trust,

Domino sugar refinery in the Charlestown neighborhood of Boston, circa 1960. *Courtesy of Boston Landmarks Commission.*

a monopoly that controlled almost all of the U.S. sugar refining industry; the East Boston refinery was closed by 1901.

The Revere Sugar Refinery opened in East Cambridge on Millers River in 1867 (some say 1871) in a building originally used as a slaughterhouse. The six-story plant could process 1,400 barrels of sugar a day. The refinery moved to a new location in Boston's Charlestown section along the Mystic River in 1918; the new plant could process two million pounds of sugar per day. By then, the Revere Sugar Refinery was a subsidiary of United Fruit Company, which owned sugar plantations in Cuba.

The American Sugar Refining company opened in the Fort Point Channel district of Boston in 1902 and distributed sugar under the Crystal Domino brand. The refinery moved to Charlestown in 1958 and closed in 1988 as demand for sugar dropped.

MOLASSES

Molasses is a thick, dark syrup that is a byproduct of the sugar-making process. Sugar manufacturers first crush sugar cane or sugar beets to extract the juice. The juice is then boiled down, and sugar crystals form on top. Molasses is the liquid that remains after the crystalized sugar is removed. Not only is molasses used as a sweetener in baked goods and candies, but the syrup can be distilled into rum. (Molasses can also be used to make munitions, but that is another story.)

Molasses was famously responsible for a tragic day in Boston history. On January 15, 1919, a storage tank on Commercial Street in the city's North End neighborhood ruptured and sent more than two million gallons of molasses cascading into the surrounding streets. The sticky liquid crushed everything in its path, including people, horses, buildings and electrical poles. Tragically, 21 people died in the disaster, and about 150 were injured. Hundreds of workers were called in to clean up the damage from

Aftermath of the Great Molasses Flood in 1919. *Courtesy of Library of Congress.*

what became known as the Great Molasses Flood, and the sweet aroma of molasses was said to linger in the air for years. A plaque commemorating the event was installed on Commercial Street, and the property occupied by the tank was converted into a park.

CHOCOLATE

Chocolate originated thousands of years ago in Mesoamerica, where the cacao tree thrived in the hot and humid climate. The fruits of the tree, also called pods, can grow up to twelve inches long and contain as many as fifty seeds (or beans) surrounded by a whitish pulp.

The Olmecs and later the Mayans and Aztecs transformed cacao seeds into a bitter frothy beverage, often mixed with maize and spices, that they consumed mostly as a ceremonial drink. Chocolate made its way from the Americas to Spain in the 1500s, although no one is certain who was responsible.

Regardless of how it got to Spain, chocolate was a sensation. The Spaniards doctored the Aztec brew with sugar and spices to better conform to their tastes, and the new drink became a symbol of status, wealth and power. Word spread to other European courts, and nations established cacao plantations in their tropical colonies to support their new chocolate addiction.

Known for drinking tea (and dumping it into Boston Harbor), the American colonists enjoyed sipping chocolate as well. Chocolate arrived in the American colonies in the 1600s, and the first chocolate house opened in Boston in 1682. Almost a century later, in 1765, John Hannon and James Baker established the first American chocolate mill just south of Boston.

As much as colonial America loved chocolate, the product would have been unrecognizable to today's consumers. Jacqueline Raposo wrote on Vice.com:

> *Packed into boxes or sold in large bricks, the gritty, fatty, oily Colonial chocolate was not suited to being a snackable foodstuff. It had to be chipped or shaved into hot liquid and then regularly stirred so that the solids stayed suspended....The melted balloons of fat would have left an oily sheen on the top of the beverage.*

Planting sugar cane in a plantation on St. Croix. *Photo by Jack Delano, courtesy of Library of Congress.*

Colonists were creative and added sugar and spices to the brew. But it was not until the nineteenth century that modern-day chocolate—with its endless array of flavors, shapes and textures—began to emerge.

A TROUBLED PAST

Despite their sweetness, sugar, molasses and chocolate have a troubled history.

Europeans loved sugar, but for centuries, it was a luxury product. That changed when Christopher Columbus introduced the crop to the Caribbean, bringing sugar-cane stalks from the Spanish Canary Islands in 1493.

The new crop came with a tragic price: centuries of sugar slavery. As the *New York Times* wrote as part of its 1619 Project, "Over the four centuries that followed Columbus's arrival, on the mainlands of Central and South America in Mexico, Guyana and Brazil as well as on the sugar islands of the West Indies—Cuba, Barbados and Jamaica, among others—countless indigenous lives were destroyed and nearly 11 million Africans were enslaved, just counting those who survived the Middle Passage."

Did you know?
Because the sugar industry was so closely linked to the slave trade, nineteenth-century abolitionists promoted beet sugar as an ethical alternative. In 1838, David Lee Child built the first sugar beet factory in the United States in Northampton, Massachusetts, after studying the industry in Belgium.

Sugar was so lucrative that it was dubbed "white gold," and it was a key component of the triangular trade for hundreds of years. Simply put: sea captains brought New England rum and goods to West Africa, carried enslaved Africans to sugar plantations in the West Indies and transported Caribbean sugar and molasses to New England for consumption and use in rum distilleries.

Chocolate, too, has a bitter history. After Hernán Cortés overthrew the Aztec empire in 1519, Spaniards gained access to cacao. As Europeans established cacao plantations in their tropical colonies, they first used Indigenous populations as enslaved labor. When newly introduced European diseases decimated the Indigenous workforce, the colonial powers brought in enslaved Africans to feed the European craving for chocolate. Today, the chocolate producers in West Africa have come under scrutiny for their use of child labor. While government, industry and nonprofit groups are working to end the practice, child labor persists in some countries.

Chapter 2

FOOD OF THE GODS

Chocolate Makers and Chocolatiers

The botanical name for the cacao tree is *Theobroma cacao*, which means "Food of the gods," and many New Englanders would agree. New England's appetite for chocolate began in colonial times and continues unabated today.

BAKER'S CHOCOLATE

The Boston area's legacy as a confectionery hub began in 1765. John Hannon and James Baker began making chocolate in a sawmill along the Neponset River in Milton, Massachusetts. Hannon was an Irish immigrant who learned the chocolate trade in London. Baker ran a general store in Dorchester, Massachusetts, and helped finance Hannon's venture.

Hannon ran the business successfully for over a decade, operating out of different mills on the Neponset. But something happened in 1779 that changed the course of chocolate history: Hannon disappeared. One story placed him on a ship to the West Indies to buy cacao beans; another said he sailed to England to escape a troubled marriage. Either way, he was never seen again and was presumed dead at sea.

James Baker bought out Hannon's widow in 1780, rebranded the chocolate under his own name and began over a century of Baker family ownership. He retired in 1804 and left his son Edmund in charge. Edmund added trading partners along the East Coast, kept the company afloat through the War of 1812 and brought his son Walter into the business in 1818. Walter took over the reins of the family enterprise when Edmund retired in 1823.

Walter Baker renamed the enterprise Walter Baker and Company and rebranded the chocolate "W. Baker," replacing his father's "E. Baker" brand. He continued to expand the company's markets, and by 1849, Baker's chocolates could be found in cities as far as San Francisco.

Baker's original product was unsweetened chocolate, intended for drinking, which the company offered in three grades. Premium Chocolate, later renamed Best Chocolate, was the company's first product and remained its flagship offering. Common Chocolate was introduced in 1798, and Inferior Chocolate followed in 1803. The latter contained ground rice and was supplied primarily to enslaved workers in the southern United States and the West Indies. Baker's introduced its first sweet chocolate in 1849 with the Caracas chocolate bar. German's Sweet Chocolate was introduced in 1852 and took its name from Samuel German, who developed the product.

Did you know? German chocolate cake—the chocolate, coconut and pecan layer cake—has nothing to do with the country of Germany. The recipe was first published as German Sweet Chocolate Cake in the *Dallas Morning News* in 1957 and credited to Mrs. George Clay of Dallas. The name of the cake referred to Baker's German's Sweet Chocolate, but even President Lyndon B. Johnson assumed the cake had German origins. He reportedly served the cake at a 1963 luncheon with German Chancellor Ludwig Erhard.

Walter Baker died in 1852, leaving management of the business to his brother-in-law and former clerk Sidney Williams. Williams died just two years later, and Walter Baker's step-nephew Henry L. Pierce took over. Under Pierce's leadership, Baker's bought out two local competitors and added four mill buildings in Dorchester. Pierce also expanded advertising and created a company trademark based on a painting known as *La Belle Chocolatière*, a pastel by Swiss painter Jean-Étienne Liotard. The eighteenth-century painting shows a young woman carrying a tray with a glass of water and a cup of hot chocolate.

Perhaps most significantly, Henry Pierce ended family ownership for Baker's chocolate after 115 years. In 1895, Pierce incorporated the company as Walter Baker & Company. He said, "They say corporations have no souls,

Walter Baker's name in lights at the Baker chocolate factory in Boston. *Courtesy of author.*

but they outlive men, and I have done what I think best for the business and for everyone." A year later, a group led by John Malcolm Forbes purchased Baker's Chocolate and modernized the company. In 1927, the Forbes Syndicate, as the group was known, sold the company to the Postum Cereal Company (home to Grape-Nuts, among other products). Baker's survived multiple corporate changes and today is a division of Kraft Foods.

Baker's Dorchester factory was active until 1965, when production moved to Delaware. The company's industrial buildings on both sides of the Neponset River, in Dorchester and Milton, were added to the National Register of Historic Places as the Dorchester-Milton Lower Mills Industrial District in 1980. In 2022, the Dorchester Lower Mills Civic Association received a grant to restore and relight the sign with Walter Baker's name that still stands on top of the former Baker's Chocolate administration building.

CHOCOLATEVILLE

Central Falls, Rhode Island, is the smallest city in the smallest state in the United States. The city has struggled financially in recent years, entering receivership in 2010, filing for bankruptcy in 2011 and emerging in 2012 after cutting expenses.

But in the eighteenth century, Central Falls was home to one of the country's first water-powered chocolate mills. (There are some references to an even earlier chocolate mill in Providence, but details are scarce.) William Wheat opened his mill along the Blackstone River in 1782. For nearly twenty years, the aroma of roasting cacao beans gave Central Falls its nickname of "Chocolateville." But a devastating flood in the early 1800s destroyed the mill, and no traces of the structure remained by 1834.

In 2010, the Confectioners Mill Preservation Society proposed rebuilding the Wheat chocolate mill and turning it into a museum. At an estimated cost of $12 million, local organizations deemed the project too expensive. Instead, the Blackstone Valley Tourism Council built a park, supported in part with a $35,000 matching grant from Mars, Inc. and its subsidiary American Heritage Chocolate. The park was completed in 2012. In addition to walkways, sitting areas and access to the Blackstone River, the Chocolate Mill Overlook includes interpretive panels that commemorate the legacy of chocolate manufacturing in Central Falls.

With the scent of chocolate again in the air, at least metaphorically, another project emerged in Central Falls. Mike Ritz, who was then executive director of Leadership Rhode Island, spearheaded the "Save Chocolateville" project in 2012. He enlisted chocolatier Andrew Shotts, who had a local manufacturing facility at the time, to create a chocolate bar for sale; proceeds from the candy sales supported Central Falls children in need. "Chocolateville to me represents the spirit of ingenuity, entrepreneurship, productivity, and—when that first mill building was created there—it was the heart of the community," Ritz told CNBC. "To me, it's the story of America in one square mile."

THE CHOCOLATE-MAKING PROCESS

Transforming cacao beans into chocolate bars or truffles is a labor-intensive and time-consuming process. First the cacao pods are cut from the tree, often with a machete, and then the beans are removed, cleaned, fermented and dried. The dried cacao beans are packed into bags and shipped to processors.

Processors roast the beans to develop the flavor and loosen the thin shells. Just like coffee beans, cacao beans can receive a light, medium or dark roast. Next, a winnowing machine removes the shells from the beans. The

Gathering cacao pods in Ecuador. *Photo by American Stereoscopic Company, courtesy of Library of Congress.*

discarded shells are known as husks, and the remaining beans are called the nibs. The nibs are ground into a paste known as cocoa mass or cocoa liquor, which is the building block for most modern chocolate confections. Sometimes the husks are brewed into tea; First Lady Martha Washington was said to be a fan.

Placing cocoa mass under high pressure separates the product into cocoa butter and cocoa solids. Cocoa butter can then be used as an ingredient in other chocolate products. (It is also used in cosmetics.) Cocoa solids can be ground into cocoa powder. Dark chocolate comprises cocoa mass, cocoa butter and sweetener. Adding powdered milk yields milk chocolate. White chocolate (which some consider not a true chocolate) contains cocoa butter, milk solids and sweetener but no cocoa mass.

The desired ingredients are combined and placed in a refiner, which grinds the chocolate into a uniform paste. A related step called conching further refines the chocolate and ensures a smooth product.

Tempering is the last step before chocolate can be delivered to the chocolatier for transformation into the final product. The chocolate is slowly heated, cooled and heated again to allow some of the cocoa butter to crystalize. This gives chocolate its characteristic gloss, snap and smooth mouthfeel.

INNOVATIONS IN CHOCOLATE MANUFACTURING

Chocolate has come a long way since the days of the Aztec empire. A handful of Europeans helped transform the bitter brew into today's bonbons and bars.

In 1828, Dutch chocolatier Casparus Van Houten invented a hydraulic press that separated cocoa mass into cocoa butter and cocoa solids for further processing. About ten years later, Van Houten's son Coenraad developed a process to apply alkali agents to cocoa solids to reduce the natural acidity and tone down the bitterness. The process became known as dutching or Dutch process cocoa.

In 1847, British chocolate maker Joseph S. Fry developed the first molded chocolate bar. (Fry had already introduced automation to chocolate making in 1795 when he used a Watt steam engine to grind cacao beans.) J.S. Fry & Sons became best known for Fry's Chocolate Cream, which was launched in 1866. Considered the first mass-produced chocolate bar, the chocolate cream paved the way for generations of snack-sized treats. Fry's merged with Cadbury's in 1919.

Did you know? The words *cacao*, *cocoa* and *chocolate* all come from the Aztec Nahuatl language. While some use *cacao* and *cocoa* interchangeably, many use *cacao* to refer to the raw products—the tree, pods and beans—and *cocoa* to refer to the processed beans and related products like cocoa butter.

In 1879, Swiss chocolatier Rodolphe Lindt invented the conching process that is still used today to refine chocolate. According to lore, he left a batch of chocolate in a mixer over the weekend (perhaps by accident, perhaps not) and returned to find a product that was smoother, shinier and more flavorful than other chocolates of the time. The conche machine, named for the shell-like shape of its rollers, uses agitation, heat, aeration and time to transform the taste and texture of chocolate. In 1899, Johann Rudolf Sprüngli-Schifferli acquired Lindt's company to form Lindt & Sprüngli. After years of growth in Europe—and the introduction of the Lindt Gold Bunny and the LINDOR chocolate truffle—the company opened a factory in Stratham, New Hampshire, in 1989.

CHOCOLATE BARS

The popularity of chocolate bars exploded after World War I. To help boost energy and morale for soldiers in the field, confectioners on the homefront donated twenty-pound blocks of chocolate to the U.S. Army. The blocks were cut into bars, wrapped by hand and distributed to GIs. The soldiers came home with an appetite for chocolate. Combine that with the beginning of Prohibition, when Americans sought alternatives to alcohol, and everyone wanted candy bars. By the end of the 1920s, U.S. manufacturers were churning out more than forty thousand different candy bars, according to Susan Benjamin in *Sweet as Sin: The Unwrapped Story of How Candy Became America's Favorite Pleasure*.

With thousands of chocolate bars on the market, the competition among candy makers to distinguish their products was fierce. Because so many candy bars are essentially similar—chocolate-covered something—many confectioners came up with unique and memorable names to set their sweets apart. Candy bars had names like Baby Ruth, Goo Goo Cluster, Chick-O-Stick, PayDay and Abba-Zabba. New England's offerings included Sky Bars, Bolsters, Waleeco, Charleston Chew and Mounds.

BEAN-TO-BAR CHOCOLATE

With bean-to-bar chocolate, the chocolate maker controls every aspect of the process from sourcing the cacao beans to creating the final consumer product. The term is not regulated but generally is associated with small-batch artisan chocolates; the sourced cacao beans are usually fair-trade certified and often organic.

Chocolate disks from Taza Chocolate. *Courtesy of author.*

Inspired by the stone-ground chocolate he tasted in Oaxaca, Mexico, Alex Whitmore decided to create a chocolate factory when he returned home to Massachusetts. In 2005, Whitmore and his wife, Kathleen Fulton, opened Taza Chocolate, a bean-to-bar chocolate company in Somerville. To capture the rustic quality of Mexican chocolate, Whitmore used hand-carved millstones, known as *molinos*, to grind the cacao beans; he learned how to carve the granite stones directly from Mexican *molineros*.

Taza's minimal processing is designed to highlight the qualities of the cacao beans. In a 2016 interview, Whitmore described the texture of Taza chocolate as gritty and acknowledged that it was not for everyone. "But the people who love it, love it," he added. "They gotta have it."

Taza is best known for its chocolate disks—Mexican-style rounds of chocolate designed for melting into hot chocolate or eating straight from the wrapper. Flavors include cinnamon, coffee, guajillo pepper, vanilla and seasonal offerings like spiked eggnog.

The company imports organic cacao beans directly from farmers in the Dominican Republic, Haiti and Ghana and works only with farmers who guarantee fair and humane work practices.

Also in Somerville, Somerville Chocolate is a small bean-to-bar maker that uses a subscription-based model (like a farm share). Customers receive bars four times a year designed to highlight specific characteristics, such as roast profile, sugar content or refinement process.

Tom and Monica Rogan make small-batch chocolates at their 225-year-old farm in Sudbury, Massachusetts. The Rogans have direct relationships with cacao farmers to ensure a quality product grown in an ethical way. "There are so many steps in growing and harvesting cacao that can impact flavor along the way," Monica said in a 2022 interview. "It's really important that we have that direct line of communication with the farmers and producers so that we can work together to have the greatest quality cacao possible." Goodnow Farms Chocolate offers single-origin chocolate bars, along with bars that include ingredients ranging from whiskey to caramelized onion.

Scott Watson was a craft beer brewer before he turned to chocolate. He founded Loon Chocolate, a bean-to-bar chocolate company in Manchester, New Hampshire, in 2018 and enjoyed the similarities between the worlds of craft beer and artisan chocolate. Watson sold his company to Rachel Mack and Sara Steffensmeier in 2023. The sisters had previously acquired a small-batch jam and jelly company and joked about creating a "jampire." Asked why they added chocolate to their jam offerings, Mack said, "Honestly, chocolate is just delicious, and I loved Loon Chocolate with the New Hampshire iconography that comes with it."

Mateo Block opened Prophecy Chocolate in Hardwick, Vermont, in 2022. He had previously spent about three years in Peru, where he learned traditional ways to process cacao and make chocolate, and then apprenticed at Somerville Chocolate. Prophecy imports cacao beans from Peru, focusing on an heirloom variety called Chuncho. Prophecy's chocolate bars include La Mexicana (hot chilies, vanilla, agave, cinnamon and heirloom corn), Wild New England (maple sugar, chaga mushroom and wild Maine blueberry) and Blue Lotus (blue lotus flowers and marshmallow leaf and root). In 2024, the chocolate maker announced plans to move to Morrisville, Vermont.

Did you know?
Although many use the terms interchangeably, industry experts make a distinction between a *chocolate maker* and a *chocolatier*. A *chocolate maker* creates chocolate from scratch, overseeing the entire process from cacao bean to final product. A *chocolatier* creates confections like bonbons and truffles using chocolate sourced from a third party.

Chocolatiers

New England has countless chocolatiers and chocolate shops. Some date back to the early days of the twentieth century, and others began just a few years ago. Here are a few of the chocolate shops that delight in making sweet confections.

Sicilian immigrants Philip Strazzula and his wife, Concetta DiMare, opened a candy store in Belmont, Massachusetts, in 1925, selling their handmade chocolates and ice cream. They called the enterprise Phillips Sweets (doubling the *L* to make the name more "Yankee-sounding," according to the company). In 1952, Philip and Concetta's two sons, Philip Jr. and Matthew, and their brother-in-law Joseph Sammartino took over the business. They bought a restaurant in Boston's Dorchester section and converted it into Phillips Candy House. Their extended family participated in the business, including Joseph's wife, Anna, and their daughter Mary Ann Nagle, who became general manager. "My dad always said if you make quality candy, they will come in droves," Anna Sammartino told the *Boston Globe* in 2013. Sammartino passed away in 2016 at the age of 103; Nagle retired in 2018 after 35 years with the candy shop. As of this writing, a fourth generation of the Strazzula and Sammartino families is still involved with the business.

Hebert Candies began in 1917 when Frederick E. Hebert invested eleven dollars in a few candy-making supplies. For the next three decades, he sold chocolates and caramels from his home in Fitchburg, Massachusetts, and then from two storefronts in Worcester. By 1946, he was ready to expand, and he purchased the former Hillswold Mansion located on U.S. Route 20 in Shrewsbury, about ten miles outside Worcester, and dubbed it the first roadside candy store in America. Hebert brought his sons into the business, and their children later joined the company.

Hebert's sold chocolate bonbons (including Classic Genevas), fudge, penuche, molded chocolates and ice cream. Not satisfied with milk and dark chocolate, Frederick Hebert also claimed the distinction of introducing white chocolate—which he discovered on a European business trip—to American consumers in the 1950s.

In 2003, the third generation of Heberts—Frederick's grandchildren Ronald, Richard, Frederick Jr. and Dianne—sold the business. But they did not leave the chocolate industry. Three of the siblings continued to operate former Hebert's Massachusetts retail shops under new names, and one started a company to manufacture private-label chocolate bars.

Jim Lampman opened the Ice House Restaurant in Burlington, Vermont, in 1979. He had a tradition of giving his employees fancy European candies as an annual holiday gift, but one year, his pastry chef confessed that the chocolates were not great. Lampman dared him to do better, and the result was the chocolate truffle that launched Lake Champlain Chocolates in the 1980s. Today, Lake Champlain Chocolates is a second-generation business headquartered in Burlington. Lampman's son Eric Lampman is president, and his daughter Ellen Reed is vice president.

Besides its signature truffles, Lake Champlain Chocolates is known for its Chocolates of Vermont collections. These bonbons are filled with local ingredients like maple syrup and honey and are custom molded in shapes that represent their home state: a maple leaf, a beehive, a lake and a mountain. Other products include caramels, toffees, hot chocolate and award-winning Five Star Bars.

Lake Champlain partners with small businesses in Vermont, Maine and Quebec for everything from cream and butter to honey and maple syrup and sources fair-trade chocolate for all its confections. The company is certified as a B corporation, which sets standards for social and environmental performance.

Born in 1872, Len Libby came from an old Maine family. After learning the art of chocolate-making in Portland, he began making candy in 1926, first selling it from his home and then opening a shop on Higgins Beach in Scarborough. Libby sold his business to Fernand Hemond in 1949 and passed along his candy-making secrets to Hemond's son Fern. The elder Hemond moved the business to U.S. Route 1 in Scarborough but kept the LEN LIBBY CANDIES name. Fern bought out his father in 1956, and Fern's daughter Gisele and her husband, John DeGrinney, have owned the shop since 2016. Some of Len Libby's popular candies are Bangor Taffy, first sold on the Maine Central Railroad over one hundred years ago, and Needhams, traditional Maine chocolate-covered confections the shop makes from hand-shredded coconut meat.

But Len Libby Candies may be best known for Lenny the Chocolate Moose, a life-sized chocolate sculpture created in 1997. Sculptor Zdeno Mayercak slathered milk chocolate over a wire frame to create the 1,700-pound creature. Maureen Hemond, Fern's wife and Gisele's mother, came up with the idea. "I kept thinking of the term *chocolate moose*," she said in a 1997 interview. "Chocolate because that's my business and moose because it represents where I live, Maine." Lenny and his dark chocolate sidekicks, Libby the bear and her cubs Cocoa and Chip, hang out in a fenced-off section of the chocolate shop where the temperature stays below seventy degrees Fahrenheit. A careful maintenance program keeps the chocolate menagerie looking young. "He has a little coat of lacquer on him, over the chocolate, but the chocolate still ages," John DeGrinney said about Lenny in a 2022 interview. "So every now and then, we sort of sand him down and take him down a layer or two, and then we have a local artist reapply tempered chocolate to him—and then [we] reapply the lacquer."

Len Libby may have a chocolate moose, but L.A. BURDICK has a chocolate mouse. These handmade treats are the signature chocolate offering at the small chain based in Walpole, New Hampshire. After training as a chocolatier in Switzerland, Larry Burdick opened a store in New York City in 1987. His goal was simple: to introduce Americans to quality chocolate bonbons. Burdick and his wife, Paula, moved the business to Walpole in 1992, and today Burdick's has seven locations: Walpole, Boston, Cambridge, Brookline, Chicago, New York City and Washington, D.C.

What inspired the Burdick Mouse? In Switzerland, chocolatiers sometimes refashioned the day's leftovers into chocolate mice for children—complete with yarn tails. After starting his U.S. company, Burdick took the Swiss tradition to a new level. He used quality chocolate instead of leftovers, and each mouse was made by hand in a twelve-step process that takes three days. No two mice are alike.

Benneville Strohecker, the founder of HARBOR SWEETS, began making chocolates in the kitchen of his Marblehead, Massachusetts, home in 1970. He had been working as a marketing executive at Schrafft's but was increasingly frustrated with the direction of the company. "I was at Schrafft's for 10 years under 12 presidents and three ownerships," he told the *Boston Globe* in 1988. "They did not produce the best piece of candy in the world. In fact, we spent a lot of time trying to figure out how to cut corners. So I set out to make the best piece of candy in the world regardless of cost." For inspiration, he asked his colleagues to describe their ideal chocolate. The consensus was a homemade chocolate-covered almond buttercrunch, and that is what he created. Dismissing squares and rectangles as too ordinary, he designed a triangular piece of almond buttercrunch dipped in chocolate and pecans. The magic happened on the day he ran out of dark chocolate and substituted white chocolate. His son said the white triangular sweet looked like a sailboat; his wife came up with the name Sweet Sloop. Sweet Sloops became the company's signature product, and Strohecker soon moved operations from his home to a warehouse in Salem. Other treats followed, often with a regional or nautical theme, including Sand Dollars and Marblehead Mints. Phyllis LeBlanc joined

Did you know?
Ben Strohecker's grandfather Robert L. Strohecker is credited with popularizing the chocolate Easter bunny. The elder Strohecker created a five-foot-tall chocolate bunny for a drugstore in Reading, Pennsylvania, in 1890. Today, Harbor Sweets honors that contribution to confectionery history with smaller bunny replicas, sold as the Robert L. Strohecker Chocolate Rabbit Collection.

Harbor Sweets in 1978 as a chocolate dipper; she bought the company from Strohecker in 1998.

Jeremy Spindler is a relative newcomer to the candy scene in Cambridge, Massachusetts, but he is deeply connected to his city's confectionery legacy. He did not set out to be a chocolatier—he earned a doctorate in musicology—but today he owns Spindler Confections and Savory Delights. He grew up in Indiana, making candy with his mother, and developed a serious sweet tooth. By 2010, he was living in metropolitan Boston, working in academia and making candy for friends, family and coworkers. He began selling sweets at local farmers' markets, quit his day job and opened his brick-and-mortar store in 2015. Spindler sells a range of handmade chocolates at his shop, including bonbons, brittles and caramels.

But Spindler also pays homage to the history of candy-making in Boston and Cambridge. He began collecting candy memorabilia to decorate the shop, taking inspiration from Cabot's Candy in Provincetown, Massachusetts. His collection grew to thousands of items, including vintage candy boxes, advertisements, store displays, signage and equipment. His shop has about three hundred items in its self-styled Museum of Chocolate and Confectionery and transports shoppers to the era when Cambridge and Boston formed the country's candy-making hub.

Chapter 3

IT STARTED WITH NECCO

Candy-Making in Boston and Cambridge

Nineteenth-century Boston had all the elements to support a new confectionery industry. The region had access to raw ingredients, a large population, transportation systems (shipping first by sea and later by rail) and a cool climate ideal for candy production. The city's earliest candy makers first settled along the Boston waterfront. But as they found success, many moved to Cambridge in the early years of the twentieth century to expand their operations where land was cheaper. Most set up shop in the area centered on Main Street, which gained the nickname "Confectioner's Row."

In 1946, a Cambridge city directory listed sixty-six candy makers. Some were industry giants, and some were modest operations. Major players included Daggett Chocolate, Deran Confectionery, Squirrel Brand Company and James O. Welch. But the biggest and the best known was the New England Confectionery Company, dubbed Necco. Today, only one confectioner is left in Cambridge. Spoiler alert: it is not Necco.

A BRIEF NECCO TIMELINE

Mary Poppins had the right idea. In the nineteenth century, pharmacists made sugary coatings to hide the bitter taste of medicine. But making the candies was tedious work, and in 1847, a Boston-based apothecary named

Oliver Chase invented a machine to cut candy lozenges into uniform disks. The machine looked like a hand-cranked pasta maker and punched out sugary disks. Chase Lozenges, as they were known, were the forerunners of today's Necco Wafers, which were then more than fifty years away.

Chase formed Chase and Company with his brothers Silas and Daniel, and they became candy makers. The candy business agreed with them, and in 1901, Chase and Company merged with two other major Boston candy manufacturers: Fobes, Hayward & Company and Wright & Moody. The three firms formed the New England Confectionery Company and sold their products under the trade name Necco Sweets. In 1902, Necco moved into a sprawling factory at Summer and Melcher Streets in Boston's Fort Point Channel district.

Necco produced some five hundred varieties of candy from its Fort Point factory, including Necco Wafers, Hub Wafers, Lenox Chocolates, Chase Mints, Canada Mints, Conversation Hearts and Bolsters. When World War I brought sugar shortages and price spikes, Necco decreased production, but the company bounced back. In 1927, Necco moved to a 350,000-square-foot factory at 254 Massachusetts Avenue in Cambridge and became one of the anchors of Confectioner's Row.

Necco's first factory in the Fort Point Channel district of Boston. *Photo by Boston Wharf Company, courtesy of Digital Commonwealth.*

Necco's factory on Massachusetts Avenue in Cambridge. *Courtesy of the Candy Wrapper Museum.*

Necco weathered the Great Depression by emphasizing the value and quality of its products ("If it's Necco—It's good!"). And in an era when money was tight, Necco's ads emphasized "full value, full weight, full satisfaction." In 1933, Necco acquired Boston-based candy maker Lovell & Covel as a subsidiary. The acquisition marked the first time Necco added a new brand to its portfolio and started a pattern of growth that extended into the next century.

During World War II, Necco retooled part of its factory to support the war effort and shifted production to electronic components. All available candy equipment was dedicated to Necco Wafers for the army to distribute to troops.

After the war, Necco returned to full-time candy production and began an ambitious program to modernize its factory. The postwar years were good for Necco; many soldiers returned stateside with a hankering for the multicolored wafers they had discovered overseas, and they became loyal customers. In 1947, as the company celebrated its centennial, 1,200 workers were producing eighteen million Necco Wafers every day along with hundreds of other products.

Unfortunately, the postwar boom did not last. Thanks in part to high sugar prices, Necco started struggling in the 1960s. United Industrial Syndicate purchased the company in 1963, and the new owners cut costs and curtailed advertising. Nevertheless, despite still surging prices for sugar and cocoa, Necco began to turn a profit again by 1972.

Fast-forward to 1997, when Necco celebrated its 150th anniversary in high style. On October 10—which the City of Cambridge proclaimed "Necco Day"—the company unveiled its newly painted water tower, which was designed to look like a package of Necco Wafers. "People had enormous affection for Necco," Charles Sullivan, executive director of the Cambridge Historical Commission, said on WBUR. "It was a local landmark."

But Cambridge was changing, and the candy makers of Confectioner's Row were giving way to biotechnology and pharmaceutical companies. With real estate prices soaring, Necco consolidated its Massachusetts assets and moved operations to a plant in Revere in 2003. The Massachusetts Avenue factory was sold to pharmaceutical giant Novartis in 2004 for $77 million; the cheerful water tower was repainted.

The beginning of the end came in 2007, when Necco was sold to a group of investors. The sale coincided with the start of the Great Recession, and the new owners were heavily leveraged. Despite competition from the so-called Big Three candy manufacturers—Hershey, M&M/Mars and Nestlé—Necco hung on for about ten years. But the owners forced the company into bankruptcy in 2018, and Necco's assets were sold at auction. Some of the company's best-known products were rescued—including Necco Wafers, Sweethearts, Sky Bars, Canada Mints and Clark Bars—but others faded away, along with the company that created them. Once the oldest continuously operating candy company in the country, Necco was gone after 171 years.

NECCO WAFERS

A descendant of Oliver Chase's lozenges, Necco Wafers were launched in 1906. The sweet, chalky disks were sold in colorful rolls of eight flavors. The original assortment contained wintergreen, licorice, cinnamon, lemon, sassafras, spearmint, clove and chocolate. Lime replaced spearmint in the 1930s, and orange took the place of sassafras in the 1940s. Each roll had a waxed paper wrapper and sold for a nickel. Necco also manufactured a sister product, called Hub Wafers, that had a transparent wrapper.

Vintage advertisement for Necco Wafers and Hub Wafers. *Courtesy of the Candy Wrapper Museum.*

Because Necco Wafers did not melt or break easily, they were well suited for travel far beyond the corner candy shop. Even before there was a Necco, Union soldiers were said to carry the candies during the American Civil War, and the U.S. Army distributed them to soldiers during both World Wars. The wafers even made their way to the ends of the earth. Explorer Donald B. MacMillan took them along on one of his Arctic expeditions and supposedly shared them with the Indigenous people he encountered. And in a widely repeated but never fully verified story, Admiral Richard E. Byrd was said to include two and a half tons of Necco Wafers among his provisions for a two-year stay in the Antarctic. (Byrd was also said to carry nuts produced by Squirrel Nut Brand.)

Necco manufactured its signature wafers for over a century. Occasionally new flavors, colors and formulations were introduced (including a disastrous all-natural version in 2009), but the classic version endured—even past Necco's bankruptcy. Spangler Manufacturing Company, a family-owned candy company in Bryan, Ohio, purchased

Necco Wafers from the bankruptcy proceedings and reintroduced the candy in 2020. Seven of the eight familiar flavors remained unchanged, as did the waxed paper wrappers, but the chocolate formula was modified for a richer flavor.

CONVERSATION CANDIES

Conversation Candies were said to draw their inspiration from cockles, a nineteenth-century shell-shaped candy with messages printed on tiny pieces of paper inside, not unlike a fortune cookie. But Daniel Chase (Oliver's brother) had another idea: what if he could print messages directly on pieces of candy? In 1866, he developed a machine that used vegetable dye to do just that. The resulting Conversation Candies were popular at weddings and parties, with couplets like "Married in pink, He will take to drink" and the more optimistic "Married in white, You have chosen right."

The Chase brothers brought their candy mottoes into the Necco merger, and the newly formed company introduced Conversation Candies in 1902. Not limited to hearts, early candy shapes also included postcards, baseballs, horseshoes and watches; messages were tailored accordingly. Necco made motto candies until the 1960s, when the line was discontinued. The company brought back Tiny Conversation Hearts and Motto Hearts in the 1980s as it sought to reenter the Valentine's Day market. But what really sealed the deal was Necco's 1990 acquisition of the Stark Candy Company; Stark had its own successful line of Sweethearts printed with cutesy messages like "Be Mine." The deal enabled Necco to dominate the Valentine's Day candy market, producing some eight billion individual hearts a year.

Spangler rescued Sweethearts in the Necco bankruptcy auction and reintroduced the candies in 2020.

SKY BAR

Necco introduced Sky Bar candy in 1938. Modeled on a European confection, Sky Bar was a molded chocolate bar with four separate sections, each with a different filling: English toffee, honey nougat, nut butter toffee and fudge parfait. Sky Bar's branding tapped into public fascination with aviation, and

Vintage advertisement for Necco Sky Bar. *Courtesy of the Candy Wrapper Museum.*

the nickel bar was part of Necco's Sky-Line, which also included Sky Pepps and Sky Toffee. Continuing the theme, the product was launched with a skywriting campaign. An advertisement at the time introduced skywriter Andy Stinis: "He writes Sky-Bar in smoke letters a mile high."

Louise Mawhinney—a retired technology executive and gift shop owner—bought the Sky Bar intellectual property at the Necco bankruptcy auction on a whim. Without any confectionery experience, she originally planned to license production but took a leap of faith and decided to take on the project herself. Because of the complexity of producing the Sky Bars—four fillings in one candy bar—she had to source custom machinery. She turned to the original Necco recipes for the candy filling and upgraded to Belgian chocolate for the candy bar component. She launched the resurrected Sky Bars in December 2019 and produces them in a storefront factory in Sudbury, Massachusetts. Today, Sky Bars are the only original Necco product still manufactured in the Bay State.

BOLSTERS

Necco started making Bolsters in 1905. The candies were peanut butter and honeycombed molasses covered with dark chocolate and evolved from bite-sized treats to bars. In 1947, Necco gave the long-running Bolster Bar a makeover—switching to milk chocolate, updating the packaging and launching an advertising campaign. To promote the product, Necco created a comic strip called *The Bolsters* about a family with a mischievous son named Bobby who always got into a jam. But no matter how much trouble Bobby caused, everything worked out in the end, and the family celebrated with a Bolster Bar and a song: "Youngster, Oldster, All love Bolster!" Necco stopped producing Bolster Bars in 1999.

MARY JANE

Charles Henry Miller started a candy company in Boston's North End neighborhood in 1884, but it was another thirty years before his son Charles Nahum Miller created the candy that would stick around for over a century: Mary Jane.

After Charles H. Miller passed away in 1888, his sons took over the candy operation under the name Charles N. Miller Company. In 1914, Charles N. Miller created a molasses taffy with a peanut butter filling that he named after his father's sister. The chewy penny candies had distinctive yellow and red wrappers with an illustration of a girl in a bonnet and full skirt.

Did you know?
Charles N. Miller invented Mary Jane while living in a house once occupied by Boston patriot Paul Revere. And, coming full circle, Mary Jane was in production at Necco's factory in the city of Revere, Massachusetts, before Necco shut down.

Charles's son Alton took over the company in 1921 and focused on promoting its marquee product. The company sponsored Mary Jane contests, giveaways and personal appearances by young women dressed as the Mary Jane character.

Mary Jane was Miller's most successful product, but the company also made other penny candies, including Strawberry Frap, Coconut Twinnies, Banana Royal and Kreem-dee-Mint. Another Charles N. Miller peanutty confection honored the company's North End roots. The Dearo was a peanut butter and chocolate penny candy. According to candy expert Ray Broekel, Dearo was a nickname for the supporters of Boston politico John "Honey Fitz" Fitzgerald; Honey Fitz called them his "dear ol' North Enders."

The Stark Candy Company acquired the Miller Company in 1985 after Alton Miller died, and Necco acquired Stark in 1990. When Necco declared bankruptcy in 2018, Spangler purchased the Mary Jane brand. Today, the Texas-based Atkinson Candy Company—home to the coconut peanut butter Chick-O-Stick—produces Mary Janes under a licensing agreement with Spangler.

LOVELL & COVEL

Lovell & Covel were the rhyming duo behind the instantly recognizable Candy Cupboard brand of boxed chocolates. C. Norman Lovell and N. Edwin Covel set up shop at 128 Fulton Street in Boston's North End neighborhood in 1900 and incorporated in 1906. By 1930, the company had 350 workers between its headquarters and a branch at 116 Commercial Street. They specialized in caramels and chocolate bonbons with names like Chocolate Masterpieces, Reputation Chocolate, The Talisman, Aristocrat Chocolates and Westward Ho! A vintage box for Aristocrat ("Service for Six") offered almonds, vanilla and nut caramels, several creams (castana, raspberry, cocoanut, coffee and orange), nougatine, vanilla dragée and molasses peppermint kisses.

Lovell & Covel became a subsidiary of Necco in 1933 and continued to manufacture candies under its own brand name. The company introduced the Candy Cupboard line of bonbons in the 1940s. The box had a distinctive homey design, with the letters of the name mimicking a patchwork quilt.

Covel died in 1941. Lovell passed away in 1949, two years after he resigned from the presidency of his company. Lovell & Covel formally merged with Necco in the early 1950s. The candy giant continued to use the Lovell & Covel branding into the 1960s; after that, the company sold Candy Cupboard and Chocolate Masterpieces under the Necco name.

SQUIRREL BRAND COMPANY

The Squirrel Brand Company began as the Austin T. Merrill Company in the Roxbury neighborhood of Boston in 1888. In 1899, Perley G. Gerrish bought the business and, over the next few years, moved the company to Main Street in Cambridge, moved again to Boardman Street and changed its name twice—first to Squirrel Brand Salted Nut Company and later to Squirrel Brand Company.

Squirrel sold salted nuts, nougats and taffies with fun names like Nut Yippees and Mint-Julep Taffy, but the company is best remembered for its Nut Zippers, a vanilla caramel peanut candy. Squirrel introduced the Nut Zipper in 1926 to complement its chocolate-flavored Caramel Chews, and it

Squirrel Brand Company factory in Cambridge, Massachusetts. *Courtesy of author.*

became Squirrel's most popular product. In a statement on its website (now archived), the company described the origins of the unusual name:

> *One of our managers came across an article in a local newspaper depicting the arrest for public drunkenness of a Vermont resident who had to be talked down from a tree by the police. When they got him down and asked him to explain himself, he proclaimed, "It must have been the Nut Zipper," referring to a local alcoholic concoction apparently popular at the time. Squirrel Brand's brain trust decided that this would be the perfect name for our new product!*

After Perley Gerrish died in 1939, his son Hollis Gerrish took over. Hollis died in 1997 and left instructions for the company to be sold. Southern Style Nuts purchased Squirrel in 1999 and moved operations to Texas. But in 2004, Necco acquired the license to manufacture Nut Zippers and Caramel Chews and brought the candies back to Massachusetts. No one picked up the Squirrel candies after Necco's bankruptcy, and Squirrel Nut Zippers and Caramel Chews have disappeared from the marketplace. John B. Sanfilippo and Son, Inc. currently owns Squirrel Brand nut products.

Today, the Squirrel Nut Zippers name lives on in an unlikely place. A swing jazz band approached Squirrel Brand in 1993, seeking permission to call themselves the Squirrel Nut Zippers. The company was initially cautious ("We were first skeptical regarding this rather unusual application of our copyright," the company wrote on its website), but permission was granted, and the band has outlived the candy.

The Squirrel Brand factory has been converted into affordable housing, and an adjacent park commemorates the history of the company.

DAGGETT CHOCOLATE COMPANY

Daggett Chocolate was once one of the biggest candy manufacturers in Cambridge and the third-largest boxed candy company in the country. Company founder Fred L. Daggett was born in Jay, Maine, in 1870. By the age of twenty-one, he was running a confectionery shop in Chelsea, Massachusetts, with his wife and two assistants.

Daggett's Chelsea venture appears to have gone under in 1894, but a company called Daggett's Fine Chocolates—presumably his next enterprise—

Making candy at the Daggett Chocolate factory. *Courtesy of History Cambridge.*

turned up in downtown Boston in 1897. Sometime in the next decade, the company moved to Lewis Wharf on the Boston waterfront, but following the lead of other Boston-based confectioners, Daggett moved its operations to 400 Main Street in Cambridge in 1926.

Daggett's thrived at its Cambridge location. The company continued to produce its own fine chocolates and expanded operations by buying out its competitors. By 1933, acquisitions included the Page & Shaw Company, F.H. Roberts Company, F.H. Dow Company and Walter M. Lowney Company. Daggett's also acquired Gobelin Chocolates, possibly in the early 1950s. In 1952, the company occupied almost 500,000 square feet, including enough refrigerated storage for five million pounds of candy. That year, the company used about ten million pounds of cacao beans and six million pounds of sugar.

In its heyday, Daggett's produced about forty brands of chocolate—as well as the boxes they came in. In fact, Daggett workers were represented by three unions: confectioners, box makers and printers. Daggett also owned a factory in Virginia that supplied the preserved strawberries used in some of the chocolates. The plant also shipped syrups and crushed fruit to druggists and ice cream makers for use in soda fountain confections.

Daggett's was a true family business. Fred Daggett's granddaughter Candy Daggett Young—yes, her name is Candy—recalled visiting the Cambridge factory as a girl. "I remember walking up the back steps to the factory and greeting the secretaries at their desks," she said. "I remember a large Santa Claus cardboard figure with a box of Daggett Chocolates in his hand." Young's cousin Meredythe Schober helped her mother, Meredythe Phelan, in the factory's retail shop during school breaks. And she vividly remembers the three-pound boxes of imperfect chocolates, or factory seconds, that she ate like popcorn.

Daggett was known to be a detail-oriented manager and a good boss who inspired loyalty among his workers. When the *Boston Sunday Advertiser* profiled the company in 1952, almost fifty employees had been with Daggett's for more than twenty-five years. As for his work philosophy, the profile continued, "From Monday through Friday, he is at the plant at eight o'clock every morning and often there in the evening. Hard work has never hurt him a bit. As for keeping young, the 81-year-old Daggett said, 'I'm always looking ahead. I keep trying to come up with new ideas. Business is a challenge, and the challenge keeps me right on my toes.'"

Fred Daggett died in 1958 at the age of eighty-seven. His nephew Richard D. Muzzy took over, but Daggett's death was the beginning of the end. Perhaps

Vintage advertisement for Daggett's boxed chocolates. *Courtesy of the Candy Wrapper Museum.*

the new executives had difficulty navigating changes in the confectionery business, which favored a few major players over smaller enterprises. Or maybe the business fell victim to the so-called second-generation curse. In any event, Necco acquired its Cambridge neighbor in 1960 and added Daggett's dozens of brands to its extensive portfolio the following year. The Main Street factory was sold to the Massachusetts Institute of Technology.

PAGE & SHAW

Dudley L. Page and Charles N. Shaw opened a candy shop at 9 West Street in downtown Boston in the late 1800s. Page had previously been a partner in Bailey's, also on West Street, and left that enterprise in 1876. He also had an active candy business in Lowell, Massachusetts.

Around 1911, Page & Shaw opened a new factory on Ames Street in Cambridge. A few years later, circa 1920, a Boston lawyer named Otis Emerson Dunham acquired the company's stock and became president. Both Page and Shaw were out.

In his 1930 work, *History of Massachusetts Industries*, Orra L. Stone had nothing but praise for Dunham and his accomplishments during the 1920s. He wrote this about the company's products:

> *Page & Shaw scour the world markets for the choicest of raw materials. Each year the company places about twenty tons of pure butter in refrigerators because it has been found that the product made when cows are securing fresh, green grass has a better flavor than is obtained later in the year. The finest white comb honey, Clermont cherries from France, the best Mayette and Chabert walnuts, true fruit flavors, and the best quality of cocoa beans are used by the concern.*

To further seal the deal, Page & Shaw packaged its confections in elaborately designed boxes. Dunham reportedly hired European and Asian artists to create the company's signature look—Moorish-themed packaging in red, yellow and blue. And those boxes traveled far; the company reportedly sold its products in elegantly furnished shops across the United States and major cities in Canada and Europe. Moreover, according to Stone, under Dunham's leadership, Page & Shaw's distribution included monthly shipments to mining companies in Peru and Mexico City (the confections

Page & Shaw was known for stylishly appointed shops like this one in Salem, Massachusetts. *Photo by Leland O. Tilford, courtesy of Nelson Dionne Salem History Collection, Salem State University Archives and Special Collections.*

were packed in "air-tight, galvanized iron boxes") and to the Arctic Circle (where the candies were "bartered for valuable skins at some of the far-North ports of the Hudson Bay Company").

Despite its roaring success in the 1920s, Page & Shaw came to an ignominious end. The company survived a hiccup in 1918 when the federal government ordered a one-week shutdown for exceeding sugar storage limits. (The federal government rationed sugar for household and commercial users during World War I.) But a stock fraud scheme brought Page & Shaw down by 1930.

In 1930, Dunham and two stockbrokers were found guilty of a conspiracy to raise $2 million in Page & Shaw stock and keep half for themselves. Dunham was sentenced to two years in prison. After his release, he returned to his estate, Lodge Pole Ranch in Beverly, Massachusetts, with $6.23 in his pocket. In a statement released at the time, Dunham protested his innocence and said, "I put all my money into Page & Shaw and, like a captain, went down with my ship."

Page & Shaw declared bankruptcy around 1930, and Daggett Chocolate—its next-door neighbor in Cambridge—purchased the company and continued to manufacture candies under the Page & Shaw brand name. When Necco purchased Daggett's in 1960, the Page & Shaw brand was discontinued. Dunham died in 1950. Today, the North Shore Music Theater occupies part of Dunham's former ranch.

But the story does not end there. Dudley L. Page went on to become a beloved figure in Lowell. Known by many as "Uncle Dudley," the longtime confectioner had a shop on Merrimack Street in the city's Keaney Square. Page succinctly described the beginnings of his confectionery career in a 1919 interview with the *Boston Globe*:

> *I was born in New Hampshire in 1845, but my family moved to Billerica, Mass., when I was a youngster. I was working on a farm there when the Civil War broke out. After the war I started in the candy business. I remember it was St. Patrick's Day, in 1866, in Lowell. I soon after took into partnership J.B. Bailey, and later we opened the present store on West St., Boston. I sold out to Mr. Bailey afterward. With Mr. Shaw I started the present firm of Page & Shaw on West St., and the concern still bears my name.*

In 1937, the Lowell City Council voted to rename Central Bridge, which spanned the Merrimack River, the Dudley L. Page Bridge. Unfortunately, the council had to rescind its resolution the following year because federal rules did not allow naming a bridge after a living person.

Page died in 1942 at the age of ninety-eight. His business was sold in 1947 and eventually became a Brigham's ice cream shop.

Charles N. Shaw tried different ventures after Otis Dunham took over his business. A 1920 advertisement in the *Boston Globe* described his affiliation with a Boston-based enterprise called the Seven Oils Company. The so-called Ointment of Seven Oils claimed to cure everything from lumbago to neuritis, while the Sev-O-Tablets relieved throat irritation ("Invaluable to singers and public speakers."). Shaw died in 1924 at the age of sixty-three.

WALTER M. LOWNEY COMPANY

Mansfield, Massachusetts, was a company town. Walter M. Lowney moved his company from Boston to a new factory in this community about thirty miles south of the city in 1903. Lowney was deeply involved in civic life and left a lasting imprint on Mansfield. He donated land for a town common, built worker housing (the factory had one thousand employees at its peak), helped create Manfield's water and sewer system and even built an airfield.

Lowney was born in Sebec, Maine, in 1855 and arrived in Boston by way of Philadelphia. By 1886, he had set up a factory on Pearl Street in downtown Boston that produced one ton of chocolate bonbons per day. Within twenty years, Lowney had added a second facility in the city (this one at 427 Commercial Street), built the Mansfield factory and opened a factory in Montreal.

Lowney advertised its chocolate bonbons with the tagline "Name on Every Piece," presumably to ensure authenticity, and print advertisements described the candies in glowing terms ("The Most Perfect of Confections"). But things changed quickly after Lowney died in 1921. The company passed to his widow, and by 1933, the U.S. assets of the Walter M. Lowney Company had become part of the Daggett Chocolate portfolio. The U.S. Coast Guard moved into Lowney's Commercial Street factory.

The Canadian branch of the Lowney Company remained independent until 1968 and is best known for its Cherry Blossom candies, which are still in production. A gussied-up chocolate-covered cherry, each individual blossom consists of a maraschino cherry and cherry syrup covered with a

Lowney's Chocolate factory in Mansfield, Massachusetts, circa 1903. *Photo by E. Chickering & Co., courtesy of Library of Congress.*

mixture of chocolate, shredded coconut and roasted peanuts. After several changes in ownership, the Walter M. Lowney Company Ltd. became part of the Canadian subsidiary of the Hershey Company in 1987.

Several chocolate manufacturers occupied the Mansfield factory after Lowney went out of business, including United Chocolate Refinery and Merckens Chocolate. The final owner was ADM Cocoa, a division of Archer Daniels Midland Co., which purchased the property in 1997 and shut down operations in 2011. The structure was added to the National Register of Historic Places in 2016 and eventually converted to housing.

F.H. ROBERTS COMPANY

Fred H. Roberts was born in Berwick, Maine, in 1855 and settled in Wilmington, Massachusetts, a town north of Boston, around 1899. After twenty-six years in the chocolate business, Roberts founded F.H. Roberts Company around 1900 and launched Apollo Chocolates with a factory on Cross Street in Boston's North End. The brand succeeded quickly and outgrew its factory by 1913. That year, Roberts opened a second plant on Ferry Street, adjacent to the Cross Street property, which doubled its production capacity. In 1913, the *Boston Globe* marveled at the company's success: "The F.H. Roberts Co. has been in existence but a comparatively few years, and is not one of the pioneers in the candy field, which makes its tremendous growth to a $1,000,000 corporation all the more remarkable."

But Roberts saw opportunities beyond Apollo and had multiple business interests in New England and elsewhere. According to the *International Confectioner*, he was president of the Fred H. Roberts Company in Cleveland (focusing on western distribution for his chocolates), president of Miller Candy company in Boston and vice president of Cox Confectionery in East Boston. He was also president of the Massachusetts Chocolate Company on Norfolk Street in Boston's Roxbury neighborhood and vice president of the Vermont Milk Chocolate Company in Burlington. His roles in the latter two enterprises are of particular interest.

The Roxbury factory produced Wan-Eta products, including cocoa, chocolate bars and a chocolate spread. A strange incident involving the chocolate bars in 1918 received front-page press coverage. A soldier stationed at Camp (not yet Fort) Dix in New Jersey found a small piece of glass in a Wan-Eta chocolate bar. This finding quickly ballooned into fears

Postcard showing the Vermont Milk Chocolate Company factory after a fire destroyed the building in 1918. *Author's collection.*

of sabotage, and the War Department was called in to investigate. The Army Medical School reviewed the situation and found the charges to be without foundation. The glass shard was presumed to be an accident, and Wan-Eta was exonerated.

The Vermont factory was established as a subsidiary of the Massachusetts Chocolate Company to provide additional capacity; Burlington was selected for its access to dairy farms and its local labor pool. The factory at 208 Flynn Avenue was designed in the "slow-burning mill style" of the time; the structure had fireproof brick walls and steel reinforcements. The factory had barely opened its doors in 1918 when Roberts scored a contract to provide $1 million worth of chocolate products for the Belgian government and war relief efforts.

But tragedy struck a few months later. Despite the factory's safety features, an explosion caused a massive fire. Three men were killed, and the property was destroyed. Describing the damage, the *Burlington Free Press* said the iron supports "resembled Christmas ribbon candy" and continued: "Not a straight support remained among them and the majority of them were wound round and round each other and twisted into all sorts of shapes."

John Walker and Roberts, who were president and vice president of the Vermont company, respectively, arrived in Burlington shortly after the fire and pledged to rebuild. The executives kept their promise, and the company survived until around 1948. Today, 208 Flynn houses businesses and professional offices.

Despite these setbacks, the confectionery business made Roberts a wealthy man. According to newspaper reports, he built an estate on sixty acres in Wilmington, complete with a carriage house, windmill, henhouse and pig house. Roberts seemed to have a soft spot for cars and reportedly had two Packards, a Buick and a Ford. On Friday afternoons, his chauffeur was said to drive him to his summer house in Wells, Maine, four hours away.

Fred Roberts passed away in 1920 at the age of sixty-five. The Daggett Chocolate Company acquired F.H. Roberts in 1933 and added Apollo to its portfolio. When Necco took over Daggett's in 1960, Apollo became part of the Necco line.

DERAN CONFECTIONERY COMPANY

In 1929, eighteen-year-old Armenian immigrant Deran Hintlian started a candy company in Somerville, Massachusetts. Seeking larger quarters, the Deran Confectionery Company moved to Pearl Street in downtown Boston in 1933. After acquiring the Murray Confectionery Company, Deran once again needed more space. So the candy maker moved again in 1937, this time to a factory at 134 Cambridge Street in the Lechmere Square section of Cambridge. The third time was the charm, and the company settled in for a long run.

Hintlian continued to acquire his competitors, including H.L. Hildreth Company (1952), Miller & Hollis, Inc. (1961) and C.S. Allen Co. (1963). The Hildreth acquisition brought Banana Splits and Mint Juleps into the Deran portfolio. (Hildreth also made a molasses taffy called Velvet Kisses, but it is not known whether Deran acquired those.)

Hintlian died in 1966 at the age of fifty-five, and his widow Anna, took over. She sold the company to Borden, Inc. in 1970. Although Deran's was no longer family owned, Harry Hintlian stayed on as president.

Deran's was best known for two products: Haviland Thin Mints and Mighty Malts Malted Milk Balls. The Haviland line, including the popular chocolate-covered Thin Mints, came with the Miller & Hollis purchase. The treats were small disks of mint filling covered with dark chocolate; they resembled York Peppermint Patties but were smaller and flatter. And while the Haviland Thin Mints had nothing to do with the Girl Scout cookies of the same name, the YMCA had an arrangement with Deran's for youngsters to sell Thin Mints to raise funds to attend summer camp. Mighty Malts were introduced in 1977 and were inspired by a Borden's ice cream treat with the same name. The candies were balls of malted milk with a chocolate coating. (Malted milk is a mix of malted barley, wheat flour and evaporated milk powder invented in the nineteenth century as a food supplement for babies and invalids.)

Borden held onto Deran's until 1993, when it sold the line to Great American Brands. When Great American Brands filed for bankruptcy a year later and shut down the Deran factory, Necco stepped in and purchased Deran's products and equipment in 1994. Necco rehired the Deran employees and set up Haviland Candy, Inc. as a subsidiary. After Necco closed in 2018, Log House Foods of Plymouth, Minnesota, acquired the Haviland assets, including Thin Mints and Mighty Malts. Thin Mints are on store shelves once again, but the return of Mighty Malts has been delayed as of this writing.

150 ORLEANS STREET

The structure at 150 Orleans Street in East Boston housed three different confectioners between 1917 and 1980: Cox Confectionery, San-Man Chocolates and Gum Products, Inc.

Cox Confectionery was a major Boston candy company with a low profile. Cox produced boxed chocolates, including a line called Romance Chocolates ("For years the choice of a selected few"). William S. Cox was president, and the company employed about 250 workers in 1930.

The company had a connection with F.H. Roberts, although the extent of the relationship is unclear. Fred Roberts reportedly was a vice president of Cox Confectionery. A 1922 Boston atlas lists the trustees of Fred H. Roberts et al. as the owner of the Orleans Street property, and a 1924 newspaper report identified Cox as an employee of the F.H. Roberts Company. (Roberts had passed away in 1920, but his company survived for another decade.)

Cox Confectionery apparently closed its doors around 1930, but the reasons are unknown. William Cox moved over to the Deran Confectionery, probably in the late 1930s, where he became vice president. Cox died in

1959 at the age of eighty-three. According to his obituary in the *Boston Globe*, he had been at Deran's for the previous twenty years.

Cox Confectionery was just the first act for the building at 150 Orleans Street. San-Man Chocolates Company took over the space in the early 1930s, moving over from 244 Commercial Street. William W. Cummings founded San-Man in 1921; he had previously been sales manager at the Massachusetts Chocolate Company (another F.H. Roberts enterprise). San-Man closed in 1941, and Cummings moved on to Shaghalian's. He died in 1956.

Gum Products, Inc. purchased the Orleans Street factory in 1943. As its name suggested, the company made gum products, especially gumballs. Wellington M. Cramer Jr. founded the company in 1940. Cramer created Yanks Bubble Gum, which was the best-selling U.S. candy product during World War II; an alliterative advertisement of the time exhorted kids to "blow bigger bubbles, better."

Cramer retired in 1968 and died in 1969. The Moxie Monarch DuGrape Company acquired Gum Products in 1971. Gum Products faced multiple challenges under its new owners, including rising ingredient prices and antiquated machinery. After three straight years of losses, Moxie shut down its gum division in 1980. Necco purchased the gum company and began producing one of its products, Old Fashioned Candy Buttons. The Orleans Street factory was converted to condominiums in the 1980s and is commonly known as the Gumball Factory.

JAMES O. WELCH COMPANY

In 1927, James O. Welch opened his eponymous candy company at 810 Main Street in Cambridge. The company introduced several well-known candy brands, including Sugar Daddy, Junior Mints and Pom Poms.

Sugar Daddy came first. Called Papa Sucker when it was created in 1925—the Sugar Daddy name came in 1932—the candy was a rectangular caramel candy on a stick. Bite-sized candy-coated caramels dubbed Sugar Babies arrived in 1935, and a chocolate-covered caramel sucker called Sugar Mama hit the scene in 1965. The Sugar family was complete.

Sometime in the 1940s, Welch introduced Pom Poms. Another caramel candy, Pom Poms were balls of soft caramel covered in chocolate.

Junior Mints are still manufactured in Cambridge, Massachusetts. *Courtesy of author.*

Junior Mints were launched in 1949; the round candies with a dimple consist of a mint filling covered with semisweet chocolate. Junior Mints had a place in popular culture from the beginning. The candy's name was said to be inspired by *Junior Miss*, a popular book, play and radio show during the 1940s. More recently, a Junior Mint played a pivotal role in an episode of *Seinfeld*. In the 1993 episode, characters Jerry and Kramer observe a surgery from the hospital's operating theater. Kramer offers a box of Junior Mints to Jerry, who refuses the treat. ("Who's gonna turn down a Junior Mint?" an astonished Kramer asks. "It's chocolate. It's peppermint. It's delicious.") When Jerry pushes Kramer's hand away, the mint flies into the air and drops into the patient. In a classic sitcom plot twist, the patient experiences complications and then recovers. The doctor attributes the turnaround to "something from above." According to the website Brands and Films, both M&Ms and Lifesavers turned down the opportunity for brand placement, apparently not seeing the humor in the situation. Fun fact: to capture the mint flying through the air in slow motion, the crew substituted a York Peppermint Patty because the Junior Mint was too small to show up on film.

Did you know?
James O. Welch worked with his older brother Robert W. Welch Jr. at his company. After retiring in 1956, Robert Welch transitioned from candy to politics and founded the John Birch Society in 1958.

The National Biscuit Company (now known as Nabisco) purchased the James O. Welch Company in 1963. Welch stayed on as a director until 1978, and his son James O. Welch Jr. later became president of the company. Nabisco sold the Welch brands to the pharmaceutical company and one-time candy maker Warner-Lambert in 1988. Tootsie Roll Industries picked up Warner-Lambert's candy brands in 1993. Pom Poms were retired at some point, but Tootsie still manufactures Junior Mints in the original factory, producing more than fifteen million mints a day.

FOX CROSS CANDY COMPANY

Donley Cross was a Shakespearean actor in San Francisco at the turn of the last century. When injuries from a fall ended his acting career, he teamed up with his friend Charlie Fox and opened a candy company in 1920. How or why the Fox Cross Company ended up in Cambridge is not known, but city records place the confectionery on Landsdowne Street in 1931 and Main Street in 1946.

Fox Cross launched its first product, the Nu Chu candy bar, in 1920. It was not exactly a bestseller. But two years later, the company introduced the Charleston Chew. The candy bar was vanilla-flavored nougat covered in milk chocolate with a name designed to cash in on the latest dance craze.

Things became interesting when Nathan Sloane bought Fox Cross in 1957. Sloane moved the company to a larger facility in Everett, Massachusetts, modernized production and added new flavors. But most significantly, he encouraged customers to freeze their Chews and smack them on a hard surface to create bite-sized pieces. The so-called Charleston Crack became a sensation.

Sloane sold the company to Nabisco in 1980. Warner-Lambert bought the brand in 1988, and Tootsie Roll Industries acquired the product in 1993. Today, Tootsie Roll makes Charleston Chews at 810 Main Street, in the same factory that makes Junior Mints—and is the last active candy factory in the city of Cambridge.

GEORGE CLOSE COMPANY

The George Close Company was one of the oldest candy manufacturers in Cambridge and turned out sweets for more than sixty years. The company was initially known for a variety of penny candies, including suckers, lemon drops and butter balls, but today is mostly associated with baseball cards.

In 1911, Close released a set of thirty cards honoring stars of the age like Ty Cobb, Honus Wagner and Cy Young. The back of the cards listed all the players in the set, and ads for Close's candies were overprinted on the text. About ten slogans were printed, including "Home Run! For Close's Butter Balls," "Close's Candies Are Pennant Winners" and the grammatically incorrect "Your Out! If You Don't Eat Close's Oppie Dildocks." The cards periodically turn up at auctions, and a set is in the collection of the

Metropolitan Museum of Art. (Not much is known about Close's Oppie Dildocks, but they may have been inspired by a popular comic strip of the time with a slightly different spelling called "Old Opie Dilldock.")

George W. Close was born in England and immigrated to the United States at the age of fourteen. He began manufacturing candy in Cambridge around 1873 and established his first factory on Broadway in 1878. When that structure burned to the ground a year later, he built a new three-story factory, also on Broadway. By 1905, the company had moved to an existing factory on Elm Street, which doubled capacity, but the growing enterprise soon needed even more space. In 1910, Close returned to the site of the company's earlier factory on Broadway and began building a six-story state-of-the-art facility.

George Close never saw his new factory, however; he died in 1911 before construction was completed. An obituary in the *Boston Globe* praised his "integrity and ardent advocacy for square-dealing." His son George E. Close and son-in-law George H. Bunton took over the confectionery. George E. Close died suddenly in 1918 of what newspapers called the grippe (presumably influenza). After Close's death, his brother Frank D. Close and brother-in-law Bunton assumed operations for the challenging decades ahead. Although the company weathered the World War I sugar shortages by offering less sugar-intensive products like chocolate-dipped puffed corn and crackers, the Great Depression took its toll. Lenders foreclosed on the Broadway factory in 1939, and the George Close Company declared bankruptcy in 1941.

The building was sold to a laboratory equipment company after the bankruptcy and was converted to affordable housing in 1977. The brick industrial building was added to the National Register of Historic Places in 2019.

W.F. SCHRAFFT AND SONS

Before the Schrafft Candy Company became known for its boxed chocolates, founder William F. Schrafft was associated with gumdrops (known at the time as gum Arabic drops). In 1861, the year his company started, Schrafft sold the gummy sweets and encouraged his customers to send them to Union soldiers during the Civil War. (Some accounts of this story identified the treats as jellybeans.)

Making candies at Schrafft's. *Courtesy of David and Caroline Llewellyn.*

The company manufactured gumdrops, chocolate vanilla creams and hard candies from locations in Boston over the next thirty years but soon transitioned to chocolate bonbons. William Schrafft's sons William E. and George F. Schrafft joined the business in 1895, and the company became known as W.F. Schrafft and Sons Corp. The growing business moved into larger quarters in 1908 and again in 1928, when the company occupied a new factory in Boston's Charlestown neighborhood. Schrafft's claimed the seven-story structure with its 160-foot clock tower was the largest chocolate factory in the world and employed some 1,600 workers at its peak.

In 1897, Schrafft's hired a salesman named Frank G. Shattuck who changed the direction of the company. After a year on the job, he opened a retail store in New York City, where he sold Schrafft's chocolates and ice cream. By 1906, Shattuck had opened two more stores, and the Frank G. Shattuck Company was established to operate the growing chain of Schrafft's shops, which had begun serving meals. In 1929, Shattuck bought out Schrafft's in a merger Shattuck modestly described in a 1930 newspaper advertisement as of "momentous importance to every lover of sweets."

The candy and restaurant divisions operated in tandem for the next thirty years. By the 1950s, more than fifty Schrafft's restaurants were serving customers, mostly in New York City. The restaurants appealed to the ladies-who-lunch crowd. In 2004, Shattuck's great-grandson Frank M. Shattuck described the ambience. "It was a much more genteel time then," he told the *New York Times*. "Everyone wore hats and hand-made suits. And if you were a lady, it was safe to sit at the soda fountain and drink gin from a teacup."

Meanwhile, the Charlestown factory kept producing chocolates and ice cream. Schrafft's boxed candy brought elegance to retail chocolates. Some products were wholesaled to smaller companies, and others were sold directly to customers with made-up names like D'or Elegante, meant to evoke opulence ("So tastefully Schrafft's," read a 1950 advertisement).

But circumstances began to change in the 1960s as Schrafft's faced competition from other chocolatiers. "Less expensive boxed chocolate brands, like Russell Stover and Whitman's, were gaining market share along with higher-priced fancy European imports," Beth Kimmerle wrote in *Chocolate: The Sweet History*. "Schrafft's chocolates were stuck somewhere in the unmarketable middle, and the company was ensnared in old-fashioned business ways."

A series of mergers and selloffs began in 1967, when PET milk merged with the Frank G. Shattuck Company. The candy operations eventually landed with Gulf and Western Industries and, later, with the American Safety Razor Company. The Schrafft's candy factory closed in 1984, and the property was converted into offices. The last Schrafft's restaurant closed in 1985, although there have been occasional efforts to revive the chain.

A WORD ABOUT WEATHER

The confectionery industry was notoriously sensitive to weather. In the years before air conditioning, heat and humidity were the enemies of chocolate and hard candies. Chocolate would "bloom" or turn gray as the cocoa butter melted, and hard candies would become a gooey mess. Even in New England's cool climate, candy making was a seasonal industry. Factories would shut down when the temperatures rose. Candy makers did what they could to protect their products from summer weather. Baker's chocolate added underground cooling rooms in the 1850s, which allowed year-round chocolate production for the first time, and Schrafft's located its chocolate dipping room in the basement of its factory. But it was not enough.

Willis Carrier designed the first modern air conditioning technology in 1902 and founded Carrier Engineering Corporation in 1915. Schrafft's was an early customer and installed Carrier's cooling technology in its factory in 1917. By the time the candy company moved into its 1928 facility, it had benefited from more than ten years of experience working with Carrier and its "manufactured weather."

Chapter 4

BEYOND CONFECTIONER'S ROW

Needhams, Bonbons and Taffy Kisses

Candy making was not limited to Cambridge; companies throughout the region have added their own layers of flavor and innovation to New England's rich confectionery tradition since the 1800s. With sometimes fanciful stories (tattoos and cannibals? man-eating clams?), these candy makers and shopkeepers added a delicious twist—and a Guinness Book record—to the region's sweet history.

NEEDHAMS

Nothing says Maine like potato candy, and that is where Needhams come in. Needhams are chocolate-covered squares of sweetened potato-coconut candy with a long history in the Pine Tree State.

The story of Needhams is a little fuzzy—and some of the details are stranger than fiction—but sources agree on the basic elements. A shopkeeper named John Seavey owned a confectionery, probably in Auburn, in the late 1800s. Around 1872, one of his candy makers presented him with a chocolate-covered coconut treat. Seavey liked what he saw and decided to sell them. But what should he call them?

Enter a man named Needham. George C. Needham was an evangelist and writer who was born in Ireland around 1844. He arrived in Boston sometime between 1868 and 1871 and began preaching at the Tremont

Temple Baptist Church. But how and when Needham left Ireland is where the story becomes downright fantastical. According to an account in the *Boston Globe*, Needham became an evangelist in Dublin when he was about twenty years old and toured in Ireland and England "with fruitful results" until around 1868. But another story about Needham's origins—quite possibly apocryphal—was reported by the *New York Times* upon his death. That story placed Needham on a ship from Ireland to South America when he was ten years old. He was reportedly beaten, tortured and tattooed by the captain and crew and then left to fend for himself in Patagonia. The *Times* wrote: "He was found by a band of cannibal Indians, who considered him a delicate morsel, and was prepared to make a feast of him, but he was saved at the last moment by the superstition of the Indians, who discovered the strange tattoo marks on his body."

Somehow, Needham returned to civilization after that ordeal and became a preacher. Once he arrived in North America around 1870, the two stories converged, agreeing that Needham held revival meetings across the United States. Maine was one of his destinations.

Seavey was likely familiar with Needham, and inspiration struck when it was time to name his candies. As Maine author John Gould imagined the scene, Seavey said, "Let's call 'em Needhams, after the popular preacher!" True or not, the story stuck, and Needhams entered Maine's culinary history. "Seavey's Needhams are as Maine as the lobster, the first sunrise, and the ayeh," Gould wrote in the *Christian Science Monitor*.

Vintage packaging for Needhams from Lou-Rod Candy and Seavey's Sweets. *Courtesy of Maine Needham Company.*

Seavey's Sweets continued to make and sell Needhams until the early 1960s, when Lou-Rod Candy of Lewiston bought the company. Lou-Rod's sold the candies under the name Seavey's Needhams until it closed around 2013.

What about the potatoes? Folklore says that Seavey's and Lou-Rod's used potatoes in their Needhams, but the spuds do not show up on their ingredient lists. An old matchbook cover advertising "home-made" Seavey's Needhams describes the candies as "chocolate covered cream cocoanut bars." There is no suggestion of potatoes. The same is true for some vintage wrappers from Seavey's and Lou-Rod's: no potatoes. (Although the Lou-Rod's product included marshmallows.)

Still, the potatoes persisted. While John Seavey and his successors were selling potato-less Needhams from their shops, generations of home cooks also made the treats, especially around the holidays, and they included potatoes. Maybe thrifty cooks were trying to stretch their household budgets by adding potatoes—a cheap and readily available ingredient—or perhaps they just wanted to use up leftovers from the dinner table. Either way, as Aimee Tucker wrote in NewEngland.com, "The mashed spuds add no detectable flavor but are as crucial to making 'real' needhams (whether they help cut the sweetness of the sugar, as some claim, or not) as the cube of salt pork is to baked beans—it's tradition."

Recipes for potato-coconut candies appeared in twentieth-century cookbooks. *The Candy Cook Book* by Alice Bradley, published in 1918, contains the following recipe:

Potato Cocoanut Candy

1 medium sized potato
2 cups shredded cocoanut
2 cups sifted confectioners' sugar
1 teaspoon vanilla
Chocolate

Cook potato in boiling water until soft, and force through a coarse sieve or a potato ricer. There should be half a cup of potato. To this add sugar, cocoanut, and vanilla, working together until well mixed. Press one inch thick into small bread pan, and spread top with a thin layer of melted bitter chocolate or sweet chocolate. When chocolate is firm, cut in small squares.

This can be varied by using nuts or fruits instead of cocoanut.

A similar recipe for Pat's Maine Potato Candy appeared in the *State of Maine Potato Cook Book*, which was published around 1950. That recipe included a quote from Pat: "A far cry from potatoes in the role of the world's number one vegetable, but wonderful if you want to pamper your sweet tooth." Pat says Maine people seem "to go for" the bitter-and-sweet combination of smooth dark chocolate and chewy coconut. The mashed potato base was said to keep the candy moist.

Linda Lenberg was a home cook who turned Needhams into a business, making two thousand a week from her kitchen in Norway, Maine. After twelve years of candy production, she decided to move on and sold the business to Malaika and Gerard Picard in 2019. In addition to the recipe (which included potatoes), the Picards bought Lenberg's candy-making equipment and hauled it back to their home in Saco on a rainy April day.

Gerard focused on the confectionery side of the business, and Malaika turned her attention to marketing. Two old-school—and idiosyncratic—machines formed the heart of the enterprise. An enrober dipped the potato-coconut patties into the chocolate coating, and a flow wrapper put each Needham into an individual cellophane package. The Picards spent so much time getting to know the fifty-year-old machines that they gave them names. "The enrober's name is Gertie. She's just a good old, steady, hardworking girl," Malaika said. "And the flow wrapper's name is Guido. Guido is persnickety. You don't mess with Guido."

But from the start, they set their sights on something bigger than simply making candy: they are Needham evangelists. "Besides making and selling Needhams, our passion is to keep the history alive," Malaika said. "We love the culture, we love the tradition, we love the Maine-ness."

Did you know? The Owyhee Idaho Spud bar, introduced in 1918, has a cocoa-flavored marshmallow center, covered with dark chocolate and sprinkled with coconut. And while it hails from Idaho, the bar includes potatoes in name only.

In 2023, the Picards moved Needham operations from their basement into a dedicated facility in a Saco industrial park. The couple also was instrumental in creating Maine Needham Day, which is celebrated on the fourth Saturday in September and coincides with the Maine Needham Festival.

The potato question notwithstanding, Needhams are part of a great tradition of chocolate-covered coconut bars (although a distinctive square shape sets Needhams apart). New England examples include Peter Paul

Mounds, their cousin Almond Joy and Washburn's Waleeco Cocoanut Bars. The James O. Welch Company made Welch's Cocoanut Bars and, briefly, a chocolate-covered coconut bar called Mr. Jones ("Two big bars in each package").

Even Necco offered a chocolate-coconut bar dubbed Need-Ums. In fact, it is possible that this was the candy bar that inspired Seavey. Necco Need-Ums once shared branding with Wright & Moody, suggesting that the candy was around before Necco was created in 1901. What if Seavey's confectioner ran across one of those Need-Ums and brought it to his boss? On the other hand, maybe someone at Wright & Moody tasted one of Seavey's Needhams and decided to copy them. The names are so similar—and candy making such a competitive industry—it is hard to believe it was just a coincidence. But without proof, we may never know.

PETER PAUL CANDY

Six Armenian immigrants came to Connecticut and created a candy empire.

Peter Halajian fled Turkey in 1890 to escape growing hostilities toward the Armenian population. He settled in New Haven and found work in a rubber factory in Naugatuck. Envisioning a life beyond the rubber plant, he teamed up with his daughters to sell fruit and candy after his factory shift ended. Within a few years, he had opened his own confectionery shop in Naugatuck; at some point, he changed his name to Peter Paul to make it easier for locals to pronounce. The enterprise was popular, and by 1912, Halajian was operating three stores: two in Naugatuck and one in Torrington. Around this time, Halajian's brother-in-law Cal Kazanjian joined the business.

Come 1919, the two men had bigger ambitions than running a small chain of confectioneries. They enlisted four other friends and relatives, all Armenian immigrants, and formed the Peter Paul Candy Manufacturing Company. The other partners were George Shamlian, Jacob Chouljian, Artin Kazanjian (Cal Kazanjian's cousin, called Harry) and Jacob Hagopian (Chouljian's cousin).

The six partners opened a factory in a loft in New Haven. At first, Peter Paul produced a range of standard candies, including lollipops and peanut brittle. To help gain a competitive edge, Peter Paul hired Harry Tatigian, a candy maker from Bridgeport. With Tatigian on board, Peter Paul introduced the Konabar, which was a blend of coconut, nuts and fruit covered in chocolate. The Konabar was moderately successful. But the gamechanger came when the Mounds bar debuted sometime between 1920 and 1922 (sources disagree)—a creamy coconut bar covered with dark chocolate and named after its curved shape. Writing in *Connecticut Explored*, Gregg Pugliese described the impact of the Mounds bar:

> *Developed by Shamlian and Tatigian, it was an instant sensation and would remain the company's best-selling and most popular product throughout its long history. Mounds was such a success that production could barely keep up with demand, especially since the work was so tedious. Each bar was individually rolled, flattened, shaped, dipped in chocolate, and wrapped in foil, all by hand.*

Most sources agree and credit Shamlian, who was a chemist, and candy maker Tatigian with developing the formula for Mounds in 1920. But another story claims that West Haven resident Vincent Nitido Sr. created the Mounds bar in 1920 and sold the product to Peter Paul in 1929. Supporting this story, the City of West Haven issued a citation to Nitido's son Vincent Nitido Jr. in February 2020 to honor his father's candy-making legacy. The citation read in part: "On the centennial of your father's iconic confectionery invention, the great people of our city join me in admiring his ingenuity in bringing his vision to fruition." Early confectionery records are often incomplete and occasionally contradictory, making it difficult to reconcile these vastly different accounts.

Thanks to the success of the Mounds bar, Peter Paul moved to a larger factory in Naugatuck in 1922 and added new products to its offerings. Amid the company's expansion, Peter Paul Halajian died in 1927, and Cal Kazanjian became president. To better compete with well-known candy bars of the era like Oh Henry! and Baby Ruth, Kazanjian decided to streamline Peter Paul's offerings and focus on making Mounds as efficiently as possible. The company mechanized its production process in the early 1930s. As the Depression took hold, Peter Paul chose not to downsize but to double down. Instead of selling a single Mounds bar for five cents, the company rebranded the candy as a twin bar. Now customers received two Mounds for the same nickel. The strategy worked, and Peter Paul emerged from the Depression years stronger than ever.

World War II brought new challenges. When the Japanese empire occupied the Philippines, Peter Paul lost access to its entire supply of coconuts. The company pivoted to find new sources in the Caribbean and transported the coconuts to processing plants in Florida and Puerto Rico. But the waters were treacherous, and the candy maker acquired seven small vessels—dubbed the "flea fleet"—to evade the German submarines patrolling the seas.

Peter Paul introduced Almond Joy in 1946. The new treat replaced the Dreams bar, which was in production from 1934 through 1944. Dreams had chopped almonds and coconut covered with dark chocolate. Almond Joys tweaked the Dreams formula; the new candy had a coconut filling with a toasted whole almond and was covered in milk chocolate. An advertising campaign in the 1950s described Mounds and Almond Joy as "indescribably delicious." But it was a jingle from the 1970s that still resonates. Liana Aghajanian wrote in the *Dining in Diaspora* project: "Peter Paul recruited marketing jingle maven Leon Carr who came up with the lyrics, 'Sometimes you feel like a nut, sometimes you don't,' an ear worm that has been going strong since it was debuted in the 1970s."

Cadbury Schweppes acquired Peter Paul, Inc. in 1978 for about $58 million. Ten years later, the Hershey Company purchased Cadbury Schweppes's U.S. assets for $300 million. Hershey closed the Naugatuck factory in 2007 and shifted manufacturing to Virginia. The Connecticut factory was demolished in 2011, but Mounds and Almond Joy are still available.

THE TAFFY PULLERS

Taffy is a form of candy made from a sticky mass of boiled sugar that is stretched and pulled until it softens. The aerated candy is shaped into a roll, cut into bite-sized pieces and usually wrapped in waxed paper. Boiled-and-pulled candy likely originated in the Middle East and came to the United States from England in the 1800s. Some early taffy recipes used molasses; most contemporary versions use corn syrup.

Until the early twentieth century, making taffy required physical strength. Workers would throw a heavy batch of boiled sugar or molasses onto a hook attached to the wall. Then the puller would stretch and fold the sweet mass repeatedly until it incorporated enough air to achieve the desired texture. The process was laborious and unsanitary.

Fannie Merritt Farmer's 1896 *Boston Cooking-School Cook Book* had several recipes for boiled and pulled candy, including one for Molasses Candy:

Molasses Candy

2 cups Porto Rico molasses
⅔ cup sugar
3 tablespoons butter
1 tablespoon vinegar

An iron kettle with a rounding bottom (Scotch kettle), or copper kettle is best for candy making. If one has no copper kettle, a granite kettle is best for sugar candies. Put butter in kettle, place over fire, and when melted, add molasses and sugar. Stir until sugar is dissolved. During the first of the boiling, stirring is unnecessary; but when nearly cooked, it should be constantly stirred. Boil until, when tried in cold water, mixture will become brittle. Add vinegar just before taking from fire. Pour into a well buttered pan. When cool enough to handle, pull until porous and light colored, allowing candy to come in contact with tips of fingers and thumbs, not to be squeezed in the hand. Cut in small pieces, using large shears or a sharp knife, and then arrange on slightly buttered plates to cool.

Edward and Mattie Talpey opened the Goldenrod across from Short Sands Beach in 1896. The York Beach, Maine, spot quickly became famous for its saltwater taffy—dubbed "Goldenrod Kisses"—which Edward pulled by hand in the shop's front window. Although the shop's taffy pulling is now mechanized, the Goldenrod still makes those kisses from Talpey's original recipe—about eight million pieces of taffy a year—and people continue to line up at the windows to watch.

What is Bangor Taffy? Despite its name, Bangor Taffy is a cream caramel rolled in powdered sugar. According to Len Libby Candies, the treat originated in the 1920s when its creator, whose name is lost to history, convinced porters on the Maine Central Railroad to sell the confections to passengers. The sweets proved so popular that the candy's originator asked Len Libby's to help meet demand. But the taffy may have been around even earlier. Delano's Candy Kitchen in Skowhegan was advertising Bangor Taffy in 1892, and confectioners across Maine were selling the product by the 1920s. Haven's Candies in Westbrook, Maine, still sells its version of Bangor Taffy, and Savour Chocolatier in Veazie, Maine (now closed), sold the sweets based on a 1913 recipe.

Born in North Grafton, Massachusetts, in 1858, Herbert L. Hildreth tried a few careers before he settled on confectionery. He began making candy in Lewiston, Maine, around 1888 and opened a shop in Old Orchard Beach to sell molasses taffy under the Velvet name. The candies were nicknamed "kisses" and had distinctive yellow-and-red packaging.

Hildreth opened the H.L. HILDRETH candy factory on Washington Street in Boston in 1893 and moved to a larger facility on Batterymarch Street two years later. He decorated the Batterymarch building in his signature yellow and red colors, and a painted sign read: "Hildreth's Original and Only Velvet Molasses Candy." Hildreth trademarked the name "Velvet" and aggressively protected his intellectual property. By 1896, he had filed six lawsuits against competitors. He also relentlessly promoted his candies ("Has many imitators but no competitors," a candy box from the 1890s read). The same box listed ten reasons to eat Hildreth's molasses candy, including:

It will not stick to your teeth.
You can chew it without teeth.
It stops quarrels in the household.
It is nutritious, healthful, and satisfying.

The Goldenrod in York Beach, Maine. *Courtesy of the Penobscot Marine Museum.*

By 1896, Velvet molasses kisses were so popular—for people with and without teeth—that they were sold across America and as far away as Australia. Hildreth was becoming a big deal in Old Orchard Beach and opened the Hotel Velvet in 1898 or 1899, depending on the source. The six-story hotel could accommodate six hundred guests and boasted the first elevator in Old Orchard Beach. Hildreth painted the gaudy exterior yellow and red to match his candy branding.

Hildreth sold the Hotel Velvet, probably in 1906, and the new owners promptly repainted the exterior. The remodeled Hotel Velvet opened as the Hotel Emerson on June 29, 1907. About six weeks later, on the night of August 15, a massive fire destroyed the Emerson and almost every other hotel in Old Orchard Beach. Some sources say the fire began at the former Hotel Velvet, but the *Biddeford Daily Journal* traced the conflagration to an annex of the Hotel Olympus where a young woman apparently knocked over a lamp.

Did you know? Candy kisses were around long before Milton Hershey introduced his chocolate Kisses in 1907. In the early days of candy making, a kiss usually referred to a bite-sized piece of candy, and confectioners chose quite creative names. Besides Velvet Kisses and Goldenrod Kisses, customers could choose among Cocoanut Kisses, Molasses Kisses, Moonlight Kisses, Elfin Kisses and more.

After selling the Hotel Velvet, Hildreth began to sell (or possibly lease) taffy-pulling machines. And once again, he was in the middle of a lawsuit. Herbert M. Dickinson invented a taffy-pulling machine in 1900 and described his invention in the trade journal *The Confectioner*. Introducing mechanization had the potential to upend the taffy industry; a single large candy-pulling machine could produce five thousand pounds of taffy a day, compared to three hundred pounds by hand. Dickinson's machine sparked widespread interest, and multiple inventors tried to patent their own taffy-pulling machines in the first few years of the twentieth century. Among them was Charles Thibodeau, who worked for Herbert Hildreth. When Thibodeau tried to patent his design, which was modeled on the Dickinson original, Hildreth bought him out for $75,000. (Some speculate that Hildreth sold the Hotel Velvet to raise money for this investment.)

The competing claims and the lawsuits they created ultimately landed in front of the U.S. Supreme Court. Chief Justice William Howard Taft

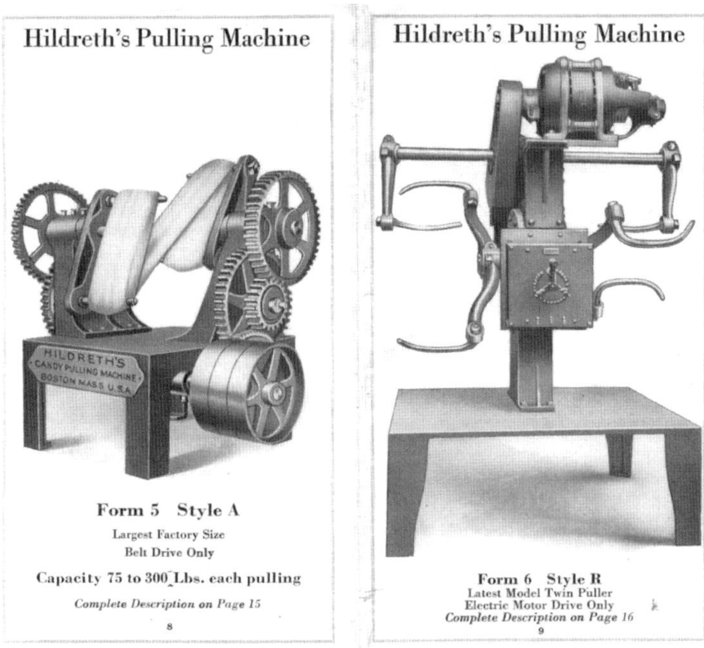

Brochure for Hildreth Taffy-Pulling Machines. *Courtesy of Barb Froman.*

wrote the majority opinion for *Hildreth v. Mastoras* in 1921 and ruled in favor of Hildreth.

Herbert L. Hildreth died in 1922. His son Herbert A. Hildreth took over the company, but he passed away in 1930. Herbert A. Hildreth Jr. continued working at the family business after his father died, although it is unclear what his role was. The Deran Confectionery Company acquired H.L. Hildreth in 1952, and Necco eventually took over Deran's. It is not known when Velvet molasses kisses were discontinued.

KIBBE BROTHERS COMPANY

Based in Springfield, Massachusetts, Kibbe Brothers Company was once the largest confectionery manufacturer in New England outside Boston. The company dates to 1843, when Horace Kibbe, who had been making lozenges from a small shop, bought the retail candy store owned by his brother George A. Kibbe and Cicero Simmons. After multiple changes in ownership and name, Kibbe Brothers Company was established around 1864. George A. Kibbe and Horace Kibbe died in 1882 and 1887,

Young workers at Kibbe's Candy factory in Springfield, Massachusetts, circa 1910. *Photo by Lewis Wickes Hine, courtesy of Library of Congress.*

respectively, and the company continued for decades without any Kibbes at the helm.

In the early years of the company, Kibbe Brothers devised a specialized horse-drawn "candy coach" to distribute their sweets throughout the region. The body was painted maroon, the wheels were yellow and the four-horse teams were white. "George Kibbe insisted that there would be never any doubt whether a white horse was clean," Orra Stone wrote in *History of Massachusetts Industries*. Eventually, candy coaches covered Kibbe's New England territory, some traveling as far as one hundred miles. By 1888, Kibbe's had transitioned to rail transportation and, eventually, motor trucks.

Kibbe's acquired the Handy Chocolate Company in 1926 and moved into the latter's Berkshire Street factory in Springfield. (The 1917 building previously housed the W.H. Miner Chocolate Company.) Once known as the "House of a Thousand Candies," with some three hundred workers in 1930, Kibbe's filed for bankruptcy around 1933.

PEZ

Widely considered to be a classic American candy, PEZ originated in Austria. Eduard Haas III introduced his peppermint drops in 1927; the name is an acronym of sorts derived from *pfefferminz*, the German word for peppermint.

The compressed sugar candy was initially marketed to adults as a breath mint and smoking alternative; the early drops were round and sold in a tin. The familiar brick shape for the candies came later. Viennese engineer Oskar Uxa designed the first PEZ dispenser in 1949. The original dispenser may—or may not—have resembled a cigarette lighter; PEZ aficionados are divided on the question.

Vintage Santa Claus PEZ dispensers. *Courtesy of author.*

European marketing activities in the 1950s and 1960s revolved around a bevy of "PEZ ladies"—young women wearing PEZ uniforms and handing out candy samples everywhere from trade shows to busy street corners—and graphic artist Gerhard Brause designed posters for the campaign in a style that evoked classic pin-up models.

Haas took a more wholesome approach when introducing PEZ to the U.S. market in the early 1950s. After determining that PEZ was especially popular with American children, the company focused on fruit flavors and modified the dispenser to display child-friendly characters. PEZ licensed Mickey Mouse and Donald Duck in 1962, starting a long run of popular culture heads to appear on the dispensers. PEZ was so popular in the United States that the company built a factory in Orange, Connecticut, to better serve the U.S. and Canadian markets; it is still the only PEZ factory outside Austria.

CANDIED FRUIT SLICES

Spoiler alert: candied fruit slices do not contain fruit. The sweets, sometimes called fruit jellies, are colorful gummy candies coated with sugar; they are designed to taste and look like slices of fruit. Like gumdrops and jellybeans, the fruit slices bear a resemblance to the traditional Middle Eastern treat known as Turkish Delight.

The H.W. Powers Candy Company in Boston was first to make the candies in the United States, probably in the 1940s. (A Canadian company called Bond and Raymond in Winnipeg, Manitoba, also claims to have created candied fruit slices; today that company operates as Cavalier Candies.) Powers sold its fruit slices product line to Vincent Aliberti in 1984; H.W. Powers seems to have closed shortly after the sale. Aliberti founded Boston Fruit Slices, which operated in Lawrence, Massachusetts, for almost thirty years and through several ownership changes. Today, Boston Fruit Slices is based in North Carolina.

Fruit slices begin as a boiled mixture of sugar and the gelling agent agar; color and flavor are added after the mixture cools. In a profile of Boston Fruit Slices in 2008 when the company was still in Massachusetts, general manager Rick Hiera told the *Boston Globe* what set the product apart:

> *Hiera boasts that the local product is superior for three reasons: because of the fruit-juice flavor made at a "flavor house" halfway across the country*

> *(he won't disclose which one), because of the gelling agent agar (he says other companies use pectin, which makes the candy stick to your teeth), and because of the egg-white and marshmallow mix used to make the fruit-slice rind (other companies simply use white food coloring according to Hiera).*

Boston Fruit Slices were certified kosher for Passover, which is one reason for their longevity. For the eight days of Passover, Jewish dietary rules prohibit foods made with wheat, barley, rye, spelt and oats (except for matzoh). Some families also avoid corn, rice and beans. The latter restrictions mean that corn syrup and soy lecithin, both commonly used in candy, are not allowed.

Boston Fruit Slices was nimble enough to meet these requirements. For its Passover candies, the company replaced corn syrup with potato or tapioca syrup and limited the selection to four wheat-free flavors: cherry, orange, lemon and lime. Hiera would not tell the *Globe* how much of his business came from Passover sales but said the demand was steady. "It's a decent part of our business," he said.

RIBBON CANDY

Ribbon candy is a hard candy with a curved shape said to resemble a folded ribbon. The candy originated in Europe, although details about where and when are scarce.

In the United States, ribbon candy is especially popular around Christmas. The candies can be produced in multiple colors and flavors, but traditional versions draw inspiration from candy canes (or perhaps vice versa): red-and-white ribbons flavored with peppermint.

The candies practically ooze nostalgia. "Ribbon candy is like one of those Christmas songs they play every year," Jim Gilson of F.B. Washburn Candy told NewEngland.com. "We might not always want to admit it, but when the season comes around, we're looking for it."

Making the decorative candy was once a labor-intensive process. The candy begins as a flat strip that is folded back and forth to create the ribbon effect. Candy makers originally wrapped the candy strips around their thumbs to shape the ribbons, but Philip Benjamin Laskey—a dentist in Marblehead, Massachusetts—invented a hand-cranked mechanical crimper in 1886.

As confectioners had access to the new crimping machine, ribbon candy became more widely available throughout New England. But the process was still tedious—workers had to cut the candy ribbons to the desired length with scissors—and production was limited to small-batch operations.

Everything changed in the mid-twentieth century. Charles P. Sevigny founded Sevigny Candy in West Hanover, Massachusetts, in 1948. About ten years later, he patented two machines that automated the production of ribbon candy.

Sevigny's dominated the local ribbon candy market until 1986, when F.B. Washburn Candy in Brockton, Massachusetts, purchased the company. Washburn's had been making its own ribbon candy since the 1960s, and the Sevigny's acquisition enabled the Brockton company to shut down its primary competition.

F.B. WASHBURN CANDY COMPANY

The F.B. Washburn story started in 1856, when Francis B. Washburn opened a bakery in Brockton, Massachusetts. The shop's most popular item was a coconut cookie, and soon Washburn tried to turn the cookie into a candy bar. At some point, Washburn Bakery became the F.B. Washburn Candy Company, and more sweet treats followed. These included the Washburn Peanut Bar and several hard candies like sourballs, Peppermint Starlights and lollipops.

In 1933, Harry Gilson moved his family from New York to Massachusetts. With no known experience in the candy industry, Brooklynite Gilson took over the reins at Washburn's and began three generations of family ownership. Harry passed the business on to his sons Lester and Robert, and Robert's son Douglas became president when the brothers retired. Until recently, the F.B. Washburn Candy Company was one of the last candy manufacturers in metropolitan Boston and the oldest family-owned business in the country.

Sometime after Harry Gilson arrived, probably in the late 1930s, Washburn's introduced the Waleeco Cocoanut Bar (occasionally spelled *Waleco* and pronounced *Wall-ee-ko*, with an emphasis on the middle syllable, according to a 1948 advertisement), a chocolate-covered coconut confection. The idea probably originated with Washburn's coconut cookie (and may have been developed by Washburn), but the candy bar's exact provenance is lost to history.

Advertisement for Waleeco Bars with recipe for "can't-fail" brownies, circa 1948. *Author's collection.*

The Waleeco bar was a hit, and Washburn's expanded through the 1940s and 1950s. Waleeco bars were widely promoted across New England. Radio ads aired during Boston Braves and Boston Red Sox games, and newspaper ads shared a "can't-fail" recipe for Waleeco Caramel Cocoanut Brownies.

Two decades later, advertising styles had changed, and Waleeco tried to get groovy. In 1968, the company held a competition among local bands to write a radio jingle for the candy bar; the winning group would get to record an album. The Flat Earth Society, a local psychedelic band, won the contest, but the collaboration fell as flat as the group's name. From the *Mojo Collection*:

> *After submitting the chosen song, the Flat Earth Society, a group of talented teenagers from Lynn, Massachusetts, assembled at Fleetwood Studios. With no previous recording experience they found that they had only rehearsed enough songs for half the album and so the rest had to be written on the spot. Time was at a premium and the studio facilities were crude, but with considerable ingenuity the results were remarkable.... Unfortunately, anyone who wished to hear the album was required to send off $1.50 together with six Waleeco wrappers. Few bothered and, with little else in the way of promotion, the record was destined to become a land-fill.*

By then, the Waleeco Cocoanut Bar was facing an increasingly competitive market. Sometime in the 1980s, Washburn's discontinued the coconut bar and decided to focus on its hard candy line, which included Dad's Root Beer Barrels, sour balls and lollipops. After acquiring the Sevigny Candy Company in 1986, Washburn's continued to sell ribbon candy under the Sevigny's name while also producing the corrugated confection for retailers like Russell Stover and Fanny Farmer to sell as their own. Quality Candy Company of Henderson, Nevada, bought Sevigny's ribbon candy and other hard candy lines from Washburn in 2019. Rose's Brands acquired the remaining assets of F.B. Washburn Company soon after that, including Dad's Root Beer Barrels.

SCHOOL HOUSE CANDY

Working at School House Candy was once a rite of passage for teenagers growing up in Pawtucket, Rhode Island. In 1912, seventeen-year-old Samuel Rosen borrowed $1,600 from his father and began to work as a candy jobber, selling candy for manufacturers like Hershey, Wrigley and Necco. Because he was still a minor, he named the enterprise the E. Rosen Company, after his father, Ephraim. Ephraim soon joined the business, along with Samuel's brother Herman (known as Hy) and brother-in-law Charles Rouslin.

The company transitioned to producing its own sweets in the early 1920s and achieved its first success with lollipops sold as Muriel Pops. Rosen packaged the treats in a cardboard book printed with nursery rhymes. As he wrote in his memoir, the pops were a "howling success." The company sold off its jobbing business in 1936 to concentrate on candy manufacturing. The growing enterprise purchased the Charles Street Primary School in 1943—hence the School House branding—and set up Rosbro Plastics a few years later. Rosbro made plastic figures and novelty containers focused on candy-centric holidays like Halloween, Easter and Christmas.

By the 1950s, the E. Rosen Company was looking for more space and purchased the Hope Webbing Mill on Main Street in Pawtucket. This allowed the company to combine its School House and Rosbro Plastics lines under one roof and leave space for Hope Webbing to continue its operations.

In her 2006 book *Elegy for a Disease: A Personal and Cultural History of Polio*, author Anne Finger described the hypnotic assembly line at School House in the 1960s:

> *Down an endlessly turning conveyor belt would flow a river of one type of candy, perhaps lemon yellow lollipops—yellow lollipops, yellow lollipops, yellow lollipops, yellow lollipops, yellow lollipops, yellow lollipops. You stared at those yellow lollipops and thought you could never in your life be as sick of anything as you were of the sight of yellow lollipops. And then you would see that the yellow lollipops had been replaced by red lollipops. At first there would be relief. Something different to look at! And then, after a few minutes of watching red lollipops, red lollipops, red lollipops, red lollipops, red lollipops, red lollipops, red lollipops coming down the conveyor belt, you would find yourself longing to see something else, anything else—even a yellow lollipop.*

Despite the endless lines of red and yellow pops, School House Candy ran into financial difficulties in the 1990s and went into receivership. Sherwood Brands bought the brand for $4 million in 1998 and moved the company to Virginia in 2002. Sherwood Brands later filed for bankruptcy and was liquidated at auction in 2012.

THOMPSON CANDY COMPANY

In 1871, seventeen-year-old William H. Thompson traveled from his home in Connecticut to Philadelphia to learn the confectionery trade. He apprenticed with Stephen Whitman, founder of Whitman's candies, and returned to Connecticut a few years later. He opened W.H. Thompson Company in Meriden in 1879 and sold chocolates, bonbons and ice cream.

The company transitioned from retail to manufacturing by the 1920s with a focus on molded chocolates—soldiers, bunnies, Santas, hearts, cigarettes and the like—and Thompson's products could be found in stores from Maine to Washington, D.C.

After William Thompson died in 1929, his son Charles took over. He briefly closed the company to weather the Depression years and reopened as a streamlined Thompson Candy Company in 1934. Charles ran the company until his death in 1951. His son George took over; he introduced automation to the factory and began wholesaling molded chocolates to major candy retailers. George Thompson sold the company in 1967, ending three generations of family ownership. Today, Thompson Chocolate is still making candy in Meriden, focusing on producing private-label molded candies for holidays and special occasions.

CANDY SHOPS

When penny candies and nickel bars were a childhood treat, many New England towns had a corner candy shop. Although most have given way to the candy aisles in supermarkets, pharmacies and big-box stores, here are a few candy shops that have stood the test of time.

CHUTTER'S has been on Main Street in Littleton, New Hampshire, since the late 1800s, when it was known as Chutter's General Store. Frederick George Chutter, a Congregational minister turned shopkeeper, was the original proprietor and namesake.

Today, the store is known for its expansive selection of candies and the distinction of having the world's longest continuous candy counter at nearly 112 feet. A measuring guide stretches along the counter (which technically spans 111 feet and 11 inches, according to Chutter's entry in the *Guinness Book of World Records*), which displays some five hundred candy jars.

Those jars contain gummi unicorns and flamingos, caramel candy corn, cinnamon drops, black licorice coins, jellybeans galore and a range of packaged candies (Almond Joy, Sky Bar, Vanilla Cow Tales, Boston Baked Beans and Pop Rocks, to name just a few). "No matter which decade you grew up in, there's something at the candy store that will bring you back to your childhood," Julie Tremaine wrote in *Forbes*. "The magic comes just from opening the jars: unscrew any of the more than 500 lids and the scent comes rushing out, and all of a sudden you remember the feeling of being seven years old, standing at a penny candy counter, counting out how many Mary Janes and Satellite Wafers you can buy with your little fistful of loose change."

Ye Olde Pepper Candy Companie dates to 1806 and calls itself America's oldest candy company. The shop offers hard candies like butterscotch drops and root beer barrels, coconut squares, almond bark and chocolate bonbons. But the store is especially known for two historic candies: Black Jacks and Gibralters.

The Black Jack is believed to be the first stick candy produced and sold in America. The shop traces Black Jacks to a confectioner named John Pepper. Pepper may have developed the candy while working with Thomas Spencer, whose mother had developed a locally popular candy called the Gibralter in the early 1800s. Writing in his 1947 profile of Necco, Louis Untermeyer envisioned Mrs. Spencer and her Gibralters (which he spelled *Gibraltars*):

> *The demand for Gibraltars increased to such an extent that Mrs. Spencer bought a horse and wagon and drove to nearby towns, selling pails of her confection to country storekeepers. Children seeing the little old lady with her ambling horse coming along the narrow rutted roads would call out, "Mamma! Here come the Gibraltars. Buy me some candy from the Gibraltar woman!"*

The Gibralters were white rectangular candies with a powdery consistency and flavored with lemon or peppermint. They were said to have a feminine look, so Pepper and Spencer set out to create a candy with the opposite characteristics. Made from blackstrap molasses, a concentrated form of the sweetener, the Black Jack stick candy fit the bill.

Thomas Spencer sailed to England in 1835 after the death of his mother, and the Pepper family picked up the candy legacy and made Black Jacks and Gibralters for two generations. In the late 1800s, George Burkinshaw started working at the company, by then called the George Pepper

Companie. Around 1900, Burkinshaw and his wife, Alice (who also worked at the shop), purchased the Pepper Companie, along with the recipes for Gibralters and Black Jacks. Today, the fourth generation of Burkinshaws runs Ye Olde Pepper Companie with locations in Salem and North Andover, Massachusetts.

Irving L. Perry began selling pecans in his shop in Belfast, Maine, in 1927. Soon Perry's Nut House stocked delicacies like Brazil nuts straight from South America and coconuts still in their husks. But Perry also had a gift for self-promotion, and he filled the shop with exotica like an alligator hide, funhouse mirrors and a taxidermized water buffalo shot by President Theodore Roosevelt. Another Roosevelt—Eleanor—liked to stop at Perry's while driving to the family retreat on Campobello Island, New Brunswick. Joshua Treat III bought the store after Perry's death in 1940 and continued the tradition. He added an albatross, a "man-eating clam" and a gorilla (again, taxidermized) to the displays. Treat sold the business in 1974, and the store closed in 1997. Most of the collection was auctioned off, but when the shop reopened in 2004, the new owners managed to retrieve some of the sold-off menagerie. Today, Perry's sells candy, nuts and fudge.

Yummies Candy & Nuts is a relative newcomer. The shop opened on Route 1 in Kittery, Maine, in 1986 and claims to have ten thousand pounds of candy on display. The wall-to-wall bins show off an impressive collection of New England favorites including Necco Wafers, Canada Mints, Charleston Chews, Junior Mints, Sky Bars and saltwater taffy.

Chapter 5

FRESH FROM THE OVEN

Brownies, Hermits and Table Talk Pies

From the chocolatey goodness of a classic brownie to the comforting warmth of a homemade apple crisp, New England bakers offer something for everyone.

BROWNIES

The humble brownie is an American invention. But is it from New England? The origins of this chewy, cakey chocolate treat are murky; some researchers trace brownies to Chicago, but a few clues point to Maine.

A widely accepted story places the brownie in Chicago in 1893. Socialite Bertha Palmer reportedly asked a pastry chef at the Palmer House Hotel, owned by her husband, to create a dessert that could be included in a boxed lunch. The result was the Palmer House Brownie (although the name came later), a small chocolate cake made with walnuts and an apricot glaze.

New England cookbooks began including brownie recipes a few years later, minus the apricot glaze. The 1896 version of Fannie Merritt Farmer's *Boston Cooking-School Cook Book* was the first publication to include a brownie recipe, but oddly enough, it had no chocolate. Instead, the recipe called for butter, powdered sugar, molasses, eggs, bread flour and pecans. Chocolate showed up three years later in the *Machias Cook Book*, published for the Ladies' Social Circle in Machias, Maine, in 1899. Tucked between recipes for Sour Cream

Cake and Caramel Cake was a recipe for Brownie's Food. Contributed by Marie Kelley from Whitewater, Wisconsin, the recipe described a chocolate cake baked in layers and frosted. It was not yet a brownie and not yet from Maine, but at least there was chocolate.

Recipes for Bangor Brownies began appearing in 1904 in publications like the *Service Club Cook Book* (1904) and the *Boston Evening Globe* (1905), at last suggesting a Maine connection. Shortly thereafter, the Massachusetts-based Walter M. Lowney Company included two brownie recipes in its 1907 cookbook: Bangor Brownies and Lowney Brownies. This recipe for Bangor Brownies comes from the 1908 revised edition and is similar to modern walnut brownies.

Bangor Brownies

¼ cup butter
1 cup brown sugar
1 egg
3 squares chocolate
½ to ¾ cup flour
1 cup nut meats
¼ teaspoon salt

Put all ingredients in bowl and beat until well mixed. Spread evenly in buttered baking pan. Bake and cut in strips.

What was the Bangor connection? No one really knows, but one popular story credits a housewife in Bangor, Maine, who forgot to add baking powder to a chocolate cake. When the cake did not rise, she served the flat pieces to her guests. The story is likely apocryphal, but a leading advocate of the accidental brownie theory was Mildred Brown Schrumpf, nicknamed "Brownie," who was a longtime food writer for the *Bangor Daily News*. Schrumpf cited a 1912 Bangor cookbook as evidence of the chocolate treat's Maine origins, but this was years after recipes for Bangor Brownies had already appeared elsewhere.

CHOCOLATE ORGASMS

Judy Rosenberg did not plan to be a baker. Raised in New York City, she attended the University of California at Berkeley. After college, she settled in Cambridge, Massachusetts, where she earned a teaching degree, waited tables and enrolled in art school. On Valentine's Day in 1974, she baked a batch of heart-shaped cookies, added elaborate decorations like velvet flowers and miniature angels and offered them to a few art galleries and a Cambridge shop called Baby Watson Cheesecake.

Baby Watson's called her the next day to ask for more, and Rosenberg was suddenly in the baking business. At first, she worked from home, dragging one-hundred-pound bags of flour up to her second-floor apartment. But she quickly outgrew the space and opened a wholesale bakery called Baby Cakes in Harvard Square next to Baby Watson. After almost three years, she struck out on her own with a bakery in Inman Square (another part of Cambridge) called Rosie's.

Rosenberg is perhaps best known for Chocolate Orgasms—fudgy brownies with a rich dark chocolate frosting and an unforgettable name. She explained that name in one of her cookbooks:

> *I still get a heightened physical reaction, a buzz, when I bite into a spectacular dessert, and lust is probably the only word that accurately describes my relationship to chocolate. So when people ask me how I came up with the name "Chocolate Orgasms" for Rosie's brownies, I don't know how to answer because it seemed the most obvious name in the world to me.*

Eventually, Rosie's had six locations, and Rosenberg wrote three cookbooks. She sold the business and retired in 2016.

COBBLERS

Call them cobblers, slumps, grunts, Bettys, buckles, crumbles, crisps or pandowdys. They are all old-fashioned fruit desserts, usually baked, with doughy toppings, and they were familiar to cooks in colonial New England. The differences among them can be subtle, often regional, and not everyone agrees on the distinctions. As Kim Severson wrote in the *New York Times*, "A proper cobbler (or a crisp or a Betty or a sonker) is what you grew up eating."

Louisa May Alcott's Orchard House in Concord, Massachusetts, nicknamed "Apple Slump." *Photo by Leon H. Abdalian, courtesy of Digital Commonwealth.*

Cobblers consist of fruit baked under a biscuit topping. There are several theories about the origin of the name. Some say that the biscuits resemble cobblestones; others suggest that the dish could be easily cobbled together. Linguistic scholars tie the word to *cobeler*, a fourteenth-century term for a wooden bowl.

Grunts are stovetop desserts made from a layer of fruit cooked in a cast-iron skillet and topped with scoops of biscuit dough. The skillet is covered and returned to the stovetop, and steam cooks the biscuits. The name is said to come from the sound the fruit makes as it is cooking.

Slumps are grunts that are baked uncovered instead of steamed. The name may come from the way the dish slumps over when served.

Crumbles and crisps are almost identical baked desserts. Both start with a layer of fruit in a casserole or baking dish topped with a streusel made from flour, butter, sugar and sometimes chopped nuts and oats. Some say that crisps include oats and crumbles do not, but many use the terms interchangeably.

Buckles are closer to fruit cakes than pies. They consist of a layer of yellow cake batter topped with berries and streusel. The batter and berries blend together while baking, and the cake develops a buckled surface.

Did you know?
Author Louisa May Alcott lived in Concord, Massachusetts, with her family from 1858 to 1877. Their home was formally known as Orchard House, but Alcott jokingly called it "Apple Slump." The nickname may have been a nod to the house's dilapidated appearance or to the apple orchard on the property.

Bettys, or sometimes brown Bettys, resemble a fruity bread pudding. A way for resourceful cooks to use up leftovers, Bettys consist of fruit—traditionally apples—baked between layers of buttered breadcrumbs or leftover cake. Jane and Michael Stern, referencing their book *A Taste of America*, wrote about brown Bettys in the *Boston Globe*: "In the traditional Yankee kitchen, a brown betty was baked overnight on Saturday in a slow brick oven, then served for breakfast Sunday morning, topped with thick cream and maple sugar shavings or syrup." The name origins are unknown, but some believe an African American woman named Betty developed the recipe; seen through today's lens, the name would appear to be a racist stereotype. Others see a more neutral etymology and think that "brown" simply was an alliterative description of the dish as it emerged from the oven.

Pandowdys are baked fruit topped with a pastry crust. Cooks "dowdy" or slice up the crust while the pie is in the oven, which allows the bubbling fruit filling to merge with the pastry. The dessert was said to be a favorite of Abigail and John Adams.

What about the fruit? These old-fashioned desserts work with whatever fruits are in season. Apples and blueberries are the traditional choices in New England, but other berries, rhubarb and pears are also popular. (As for the sonker that received a *New York Times* mention, it is a strictly southern concoction of stewed fruit or sweet potatoes.)

ELECTION DAY CAKE

Americans celebrated voting with great fanfare in the eighteenth and nineteenth centuries. Many of New England's early settlers were Puritans who rejected religious holidays like Christmas and Easter. Instead, they created their own secular celebrations, and Election Day was one of the biggest. Suffrage was limited to white male property holders in the earliest days of the country (and colonial rule before that), and the wealthy men who had the privilege of voting took part in lavish public celebrations with plenty of food and drink.

The tradition of serving a special cake on Election Day began sometime in the late 1700s. Election Day Cake (sometimes called Hartford Election Day Cake) is a pastry filled with fruit and nuts. Food historian Stephen Schmidt traced the cake to 1771, when records for the Connecticut colony's Election Day expenditures included reimbursement for what was likely a very large cake.

Early cookbook author Amelia Simmons is credited with popularizing Election Cake. She included a recipe for the cake in the second edition of her book *American Cookery*, published in 1800. The recipe made enough cake to feed a crowd and called for ten pounds of butter, fourteen pounds of sugar and twelve pounds of raisins.

Nearly a century later, Fannie Merritt Farmer included a recipe for Election Cake in the *Boston Cooking-School Cook Book*. By Farmer's time, the recipe had shrunk to what would be considered modern proportions. Instead of ten pounds of butter, her recipe called for just one-half cup.

Election Cake

½ cup butter
1 cup bread dough
1 egg
1 cup brown sugar
½ cup sour milk
⅔ cup raisins seeded, and cut in pieces
8 finely chopped figs
1 ¼ cups flour
½ teaspoon soda
1 teaspoon cinnamon
¼ teaspoon clove
¼ teaspoon mace
¼ teaspoon nutmeg
1 teaspoon salt

Work butter into dough, using the hand. Add egg well beaten, sugar, milk, fruit dredged with two tablespoons flour, and flour mixed and sifted with remaining ingredients. Put into a well-buttered bread pan, cover, and let rise one and one-fourth hours. Bake one hour in a slow oven. Cover with Boiled Milk Frosting.

In recent years, some parties have tried to revive the tradition of Election Day Cake. In 2016, a group of bakers encouraged chefs to reinvent the historical cake and coined the hashtag #MakeAmericaCakeAgain. And the cake returned to its Hartford origins in 2022. The Connecticut Old State House hosted an Election Cake bakeoff, inviting chefs to create modern interpretations of the traditional spice cake.

INDIAN PUDDING

Some consider Indian pudding to be America's first dessert. The sweetened and baked cornmeal porridge dates to the seventeenth century; colonial cooks were probably trying to use local ingredients to re-create hasty pudding, a dish they knew from England. Hasty pudding combined wheat

Durgin-Park was known for Yankee comfort foods, including Indian Pudding. *Courtesy of author.*

flour or oats with milk or water into a thickened gruel. With neither flour nor oats readily available, colonial cooks used cornmeal, which they called "Indian meal." They sweetened the dish with molasses and sometimes added nutmeg and ginger.

Many Bostonians associate Indian pudding with Durgin-Park. Established in 1827 (and closed in 2019), the restaurant served traditional Yankee comfort food at long communal tables; the Indian pudding was served warm with a scoop of vanilla ice cream.

Some modern cooks consider the name *Indian pudding* to be culturally insensitive. The *New York Times*, among other recipe sources, has renamed the dish Puritan Pudding, but the ingredients have not changed.

JOE FROGGERS

Joseph Brown was born into slavery in 1750, the son of an African American mother and a Wampanoag father. He served in the Revolutionary War, enlisting in a militia in Marblehead, Massachusetts, and may have been freed for his service. His wife, Lucretia Thomas Brown, was born in Marblehead in 1772; she was the daughter of two freed slaves.

In 1795, the Browns bought a home on Gingerbread Hill, where they opened a tavern called Black Joe's. "Marblehead was once a rough and tumble seaport," Julia Blakely wrote in *Smithsonian Magazine*. "Fishermen, sailors and other workers marginalized in the Puritan society would gather at the integrated 'Black Joe's' tavern for drinking, dancing and gambling." Plate-sized molasses-spice cookies flavored with rum were also on the menu.

Most stories credit Lucretia, sometimes called Aunt Crese, with developing the giant cookies known as Joe Froggers. The name is a bit of a mystery but may refer to the size of the lily pads in the millpond next to the tavern—or perhaps to the frogs themselves. Because the rum acted as a preservative, the cookies were popular with local fishermen heading out for long voyages.

Joe Frogger cookies have had a recent resurgence. The cookies were featured at the National Museum of African American History and Culture's Sweet Home Café. Martha Stewart published an updated recipe for Joe Froggers that she called Pumpkin-Shaped Molasses Spice Cookies in 2023. And the cookies are available for purchase at Old Sturbridge Village in Massachusetts.

Today, Black Joe's Tavern is a private residence.

JORDAN MARSH BLUEBERRY MUFFINS

Jordan Marsh was a New England department store chain with a flagship location in downtown Boston. Founded by Eben Jordan and Benjamin Marsh in 1851, the store introduced the concept of "department shopping" and was one of the first to have electric lights and elevators. But many people remember Jordan Marsh for one thing: its legendary blueberry muffins.

The large cakey muffins had a crispy sugary top and were bursting with berries. Food writer Sheryl Julian described their appeal in the *Boston Globe* in 1998: "Jordan Marsh blueberry muffins were a Bostonian's answer to Marcel Proust's madeleines. And like the little French cakes immortalized in Proust's memoir, Jordan's berry-filled muffins, still warm after an eager child's trolley ride into town to fetch them, can release floodgates of lost memories."

John Pupek began working at Jordan Marsh in 1961. Nicknamed the Muffin Man, he made the store's blueberry muffins for thirty years. After retiring, he served as a consultant to Montilio's Baking Company, which makes the Jordan Marsh blueberry muffins from the original recipe. (Macy's acquired Jordan Marsh in 1994.)

What made the muffins so special? Pupek shared his secrets on a Boston news program:

- Use a blend of bread and pastry flour.
- Flour the blueberries before mixing.
- Don't forget to drain the berries.
- Fill the muffin tins totally full.
- Put a fistful of sugar on top.

Recipes for Jordan Marsh blueberry muffins have circulated for years. They were published in local newspapers, and handwritten versions were passed down from mothers to daughters. This version appeared in the *Boston Globe* in 1974:

"Marshy" Muffins

½ cup butter
1 cup sugar
2 eggs
2 cups flour (unsifted)
2 teaspoons baking powder
½ teaspoon salt
½ cup milk
1 teaspoon vanilla
2½ cups blueberries
2 teaspoons sugar for top

On low speed of mixer, cream butter and sugar until fluffy. Add eggs, one at a time, and mix until blended. Sift flour, baking powder and salt and add alternately with milk and vanilla.

Mash ½ cup of the berries and stir in with rest of berries by hand. Grease muffin tins well with butter and grease top surface of pans as well. Pile mix high in each muffin cup. Sprinkle the 2 teaspoons sugar over tops. Bake at 375 degrees for 30 minutes. Cool in pan at least 30 minutes before serving. Makes about 12 muffins.

The recipe came with a warning that the formula only approximated the genuine Jordan Marsh recipe. The actual recipe was geared for commercial production and used a special blend of flours.

HERMITS

Hermits are traditional bar cookies loaded with spices and studded with raisins or currants. Early recipes called for nutmeg, cloves and cinnamon; bakers used white sugar, brown sugar or molasses to sweeten the chewy cookies. Modern recipes often add nuts and dried fruits like cranberries or dates. The cookies kept well, which made them popular with sailors and travelers.

Like many traditional New England treats, the exact origins of hermit cookies are a little fuzzy. The earliest printed recipes date from the late nineteenth century in the Champlain Valley; early cookbooks printed in Vermont and Upstate New York both include the cookies. The name *hermit* is also a mystery. But writing in the *Springfield Daily Republican* in 1888, author and educator Anna Burrows shared detailed advice for enjoying a picnic, including this recipe for hermits and a possible explanation for their name:

> *Quite as good as fruit cake are the cookies called "hermits." To any rich cookie dough add one teaspoonful mixed spice—clove, cinnamon and allspice—and one solid cup-ful of chopped fruit, either citron, currants, seeded raisins, or a mixture of all. Roll and bake like cookies, but rather thicker. These will keep months if out of humanity's reach, hence, perhaps their name.*

Generations of Bostonians remember the blueberry muffins from Jordan Marsh. *Courtesy of City of Boston Archives.*

Others have suggested that the cookies were once made in religious hermitages or, alternatively, the russet color of the cookies resembled the brown robes worn by hermits.

TABLE TALK PIES

Theodore Tonna and Angelo Cotsidas opened a bakery in Worcester, Massachusetts, in 1924. The pair of Greek immigrants first sold bread but soon added pies to their offerings. They called their new pies Table Talk, ostensibly to evoke an image of conversations around the kitchen table, but family lore suggests the name was also based on Tonna's initials.

After years of pie production and corporate expansion, Table Talk's owners were ready to retire in the 1960s. Without a family member willing to take over, Table Talk was sold to Beech-Nut in 1965. Tonno's son-in-law Christos Cocaine (an awkward Americanization of his family name Kokkinis) stayed on with the company after the sale.

Things began to go downhill for Table Talk, and the company shut down in 1984. Cocaine had already left the company in 1977, but he stayed in the picture. He bought Table Talk out of bankruptcy in 1985 and reopened the bakery in 1986.

The revived company focused on producing snack pies—four-inch pies that were sold mostly to grocery and convenience stores—and soon Table Talk pies were seemingly everywhere. "It was just a great lunch pail desert," Cocaine's son Harry Kokkinis recalled. "So many people would talk about how their mothers would put the junior pie in their lunchbox every day."

Harry Kokkinis began working at Table Talk in 2003 and took over as CEO after Cocaine passed away in 2015. He stepped down in 2023, and Table Talk was acquired by Minnesota-based Rise Bakery Co. in 2024, ending almost a century of family ownership.

Table Talk has been making pies in Worcester, Massachusetts, since 1924. *Courtesy of author.*

GRAPE-NUT PUDDING

There are no grapes in Grape-Nuts cereal; neither are there nuts. Instead, Grape-Nuts are crunchy nuggets of wheat and barley introduced by Charles W. Post in 1897. (It is likely that Post stole the recipe from the Kellogg brothers of corn flake fame, but that is another story entirely.)

Regardless of their questionable origins, Grape-Nuts quickly became popular, and home cooks incorporated them into all sorts of dishes. Grape-Nut pudding was one of them—a vanilla custard, usually spiced with cinnamon and nutmeg, with a layer of softened Grape-Nuts cereal at the bottom. The dish is pure comfort food (much like its frozen cousin: Grape-Nut ice cream).

And while the cereal itself has no apparent history in New England, Grape-Nut pudding somehow became a beloved regional dessert. A recipe for the pudding appeared in a cookbook published by the Dudley Street Baptist Church in Boston in 1901, cementing the New England connection, which remains strong to this day.

Chapter 6

OUT OF THE FRYER

From Doughnuts to Doughboys

Who can resist the allure of fried dough? From doughnuts and doughboys to cannoli and zeppole, New England bakeries are brimming with delicious options.

WHO PUT THE HOLE IN THE DOUGHNUT?

Starting with the basics, doughnuts (also spelled *donuts*) are deep-fried pieces of dough, usually sweetened and typically ring-shaped. Most doughnuts fall into one of two categories, yeast or cake, although the variations in flavors, fillings and toppings are limited only by the imagination of the baker. Yeast doughnuts, also called raised doughnuts, are leavened with yeast. (Brioche doughnuts are a richer version of raised doughnuts.) Cake doughnuts are leavened with baking powder or soda and tend to be denser than their yeast-raised counterparts. The batter for cake doughnuts may be flavored, whereas yeast doughnuts usually take their flavor from the icing or the filling. (Jelly doughnuts are yeasted.)

While not unique to New England, cider doughnuts are a beloved regional treat. The cakey delicacies include apple cider and spices like nutmeg and cinnamon in the batter; some bakers also incorporate apple pieces. They are usually sprinkled with sugar and are best enjoyed straight from the fryer with a glass of fresh-pressed cider on a crisp autumn day.

Above: Baker's Chocolate introduced its La Belle Chocolatière logo in 1877. *Courtesy of Digital Commonwealth.*

Left: Vintage trade card to promote Bailey's candies. *Courtesy of Library of Congress.*

Above: Elaborate box for Apollo Chocolates. *Courtesy of author.*

Left: Vintage trade card from Baker's Chocolate with artist's rendering of a cacao pod. *Courtesy of Digital Commonwealth.*

Right: Newport Creamery's signature Awful Awful ice cream drink. *Courtesy of author.*

Below: Boston Cream Pie is the official state pie of Massachusetts. *Courtesy of Omni Parker House.*

Left: Fresh batch of cider doughnuts at Applecrest Farm Orchards. *Courtesy of author.*

Below: The famous Chocolate Orgasms at Rosie's Bakery. *Courtesy of Judy Rosenberg.*

Above: Creemees are everywhere in Vermont. *Courtesy of author.*

Left: Dairy Creme in Montpelier, Vermont. *Courtesy of author.*

Right: Hebert Candy Mansion in Shrewsbury, Massachusetts. *Photo by John Margolies, courtesy of Library of Congress.*

Below: The sunny yellow sign at Village Creeme Stand in Bristol, Vermont. *Courtesy of author.*

Top: Chocolate truffles from Lake Champlain Chocolates. *Courtesy of Lake Champlain Chocolates.*

Middle: Needhams are a historic treat from the state of Maine. *Courtesy of Maine Needham Company*.

Bottom: A traditional whoopie pie has two mounds of chocolate cake with a creamy white filling. *Courtesy of author*.

Above: The Center Theatre welcomes visitors to the annual Whoopie Pie Festival in Dover-Foxcroft, Maine. *Courtesy of author.*

Left: A box of colorful Sevigny's Ribbon Candy. *Courtesy of author*.

Left: Squirrel Brand gained fame with its Nut Zippers. *Courtesy of History Cambridge.*

Below: Tubs of Marshmallow Fluff. *Courtesy of author.*

Above: Vintage advertising card for Velvet Kisses molasses taffy. *Courtesy of Barb Froman.*

Left: Vintage advertisement for Schrafft's chocolate bars. *Courtesy of David and Caroline Llewellyn.*

Left: Advertisement for Peter Paul Mounds and Almond Joy. *Author's collection.*

Below: The Page & Shaw factory in Cambridge, Massachusetts. *Author's collection.*

Above: Vintage matchbook cover advertising Waleeco Cocoanut Bars. *Author's collection.*

Left: Charles N. Miller named Mary Jane candy after his favorite aunt. *Courtesy of the Candy Wrapper Museum.*

Right: Vintage matchbook cover from Lou-Rod Candy advertising Seavey's Cocoanut Needhams. *Author's collection.*

Above: Necco created a comic strip to advertise its Bolster candies. *Courtesy of the Candy Wrapper Museum*.

Left: Workers painting the Necco water tower in 1986. *Photo by Phil Barber.*

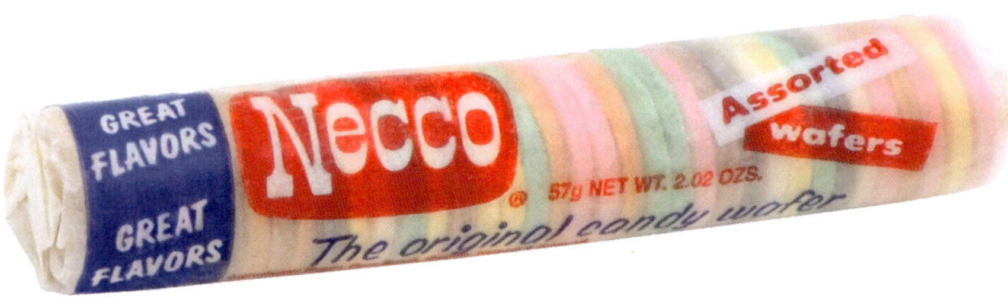

Top: Conversation Candies offered romance on a budget. *Courtesy of David and Caroline Llewellyn.*

Bottom: Necco Wafers started a candy dynasty. *Courtesy of the Candy Wrapper Museum.*

Vintage Necco labels. *Courtesy of Jeff Green.*

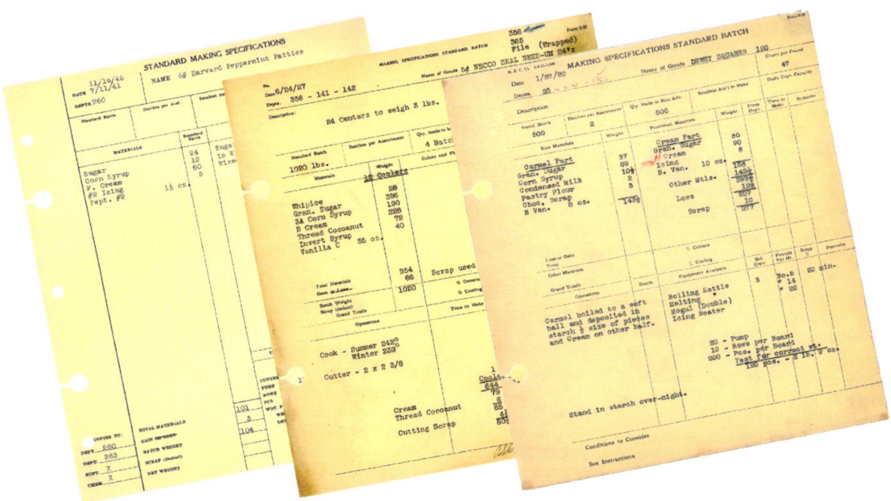

Necco recipe specifications for Harvard Peppermint Patties, Need-Ums and Dewey Squares. *Courtesy of Jeff Green.*

Left: The Berwick Cake Company in Boston began making whoopie pies in the 1920s. *Courtesy of Boston Real Estate Collaborative LLC.*

Below: Box for Lovell & Covel Candy Cupboard Chocolates. *Courtesy of the Candy Wrapper Museum.*

Dutch colonists probably brought doughnuts with them when they arrived in New Amsterdam (now Manhattan) in the seventeenth century. They called the fried confections *olykoeks*, and the so-called oily cakes did not have holes.

No one really knows when or why doughnuts acquired holes, but many attribute the innovation to a New England sea captain. Hanson Crockett Gregory was born in Rockport, Maine, in 1832. He went to sea as a teenager and made his contribution to culinary history in 1847. He told his story to reporters in 1916. "Now in them days we used to cut the doughnuts into diamond shapes and also into long strips, bent in half, and then twisted," he began. The problem was that the fried dough was properly cooked along the edges but nearly raw in the center. Then came what he called a "great inspiration"—why not cut out the troublesome centers? He said, "I took the cover off the ship's tin pepper box, and I cut into the middle of that doughnut the first hole ever seen by mortal eyes!"

Not everyone believed Gregory's oft-repeated tale, and the National Dunking Association convened a panel in 1941 to settle the matter once and for all. Fred Crockett presented the case for his ancestor Captain Gregory. The counter-argument came from Chief High Eagle of the Mashpee Wampanoag tribe; he said that one of his wife's ancestors had shot an arrow at a Pilgrim woman but punctured her fried dough cake instead. Henry A. Ellis, a Cape Cod lawyer, also supported the arrow theory. The group voted three to one to accept Crockett's seafaring tale, and Ellis eventually admitted that he made up the arrow story.

In 1947, a small monument was erected at Gregory's birthplace in Rockport, and the town hosts an annual doughnut festival to honor its native son. Gregory passed away in 1921. He lived out his final years at Sailors' Snug Harbor, a retirement home in Quincy, Massachusetts—the same city where Dunkin' Donuts was founded a few decades later.

DUNKIN' DONUTS

In 1948, an eighth-grade dropout named Bill Rosenberg opened a restaurant called Open Kettle in Quincy, Massachusetts. Two years later, he renamed the spot Dunkin' Donuts, and a coffee-and-doughnut empire was born.

After opening five additional locations, the company transitioned to a franchise model in 1955. Rosenberg was a hands-on executive and worked

The first Dunkin' Donuts opened in Quincy, Massachusetts, in 1950. *Courtesy of Dunkin' Donuts.*

Mister Donut and Dunkin' Donuts were owned by estranged brothers-in-law and competed for years. *Photo by John Margolies, courtesy of Library of Congress.*

closely with the franchise owners. "When they see me coming they say, 'Oh oh…trouble,'" he told the *Boston Globe* in 1964. "But what would be the good of traveling around just to slap backs? I want to pass on the benefits of franchising, keep them efficient, prevent them from making the same old mistakes. They make money, I make money. It's as simple as that."

In 1963, Rosenberg asked his son Robert to become CEO of Universal Food Systems, which was a group of eight small food businesses, including Dunkin' Donuts. Bob Rosenberg was just twenty-five years old at the time with a newly minted MBA from Harvard Business School but limited management experience. Once he took over, Rosenberg decided to focus on Dunkin' Donuts.

In the first five years of his tenure, Rosenberg standardized the menu, setup and pricing for the Dunkin' Donuts franchises and expanded into new markets. The strategy worked, and the chain grew from about 100 stores to almost 300. The other businesses in the Universal Food Systems portfolio closed or were sold off, and the company was renamed Dunkin' Donuts. The company went public in 1968 and was acquired by Allied-Lyons (which also owned Baskin-Robbins) in 1990 after fending off a hostile takeover attempt. Dunkin' Donuts and Baskin-Robbins (operating as Dunkin' Brands) were sold to a consortium of private equity investors in 2005, and Dunkin' Brands became part of Inspire Brands in 2020. Today, Dunkin' (Donuts was dropped from the name in 2019) describes itself as the "largest coffee and donuts brand in the United States" and has more than 13,200 restaurants around the world.

Did you know? Bill Rosenberg and Harry Winokur were brothers-in-law and business partners in the early years of Dunkin' Donuts, but they had a falling out. Rosenberg bought out Winokur in 1955, and the latter used the proceeds to establish the Mister Donut chain. The two doughnut giants competed until Dunkin's parent company acquired Mister Donut in 1990.

Despite its global presence, the brand has a particular connection with New England—especially Boston. The company doubles down on this affinity by supporting New England's professional sports teams—even launching a limited-edition doughnut inspired by the New England Patriots in 2021—and ads feature Boston celebrities like Ben Affleck and Matt Damon. But the connection extends beyond red and blue sprinkles. Many New Englanders identify with Dunkin' Donuts. "While other chains assume a national identity, forsaking the local, Dunkin' Donuts continues to be perceived by New Englanders as a local coffee shop, deserving of community patronage and support," Emily Contois wrote in the *Inquisitive Eater*. "Furthermore, Dunkin' Donuts honors not only its roots, but also the hard-working people of New England by maintaining a proud and genuine working class identity."

DOUGHNUT SHOPS AND FARMSTANDS

Doughnuts are widely available throughout New England, traditionally at storefronts and farmstands but also at supermarkets, convenience stores and even gas stations. And while Dunkin' Donuts may be a national player, albeit with Massachusetts roots, the region has plenty of independent proprietors with devoted followings. A small sampling of the region's doughnut shops and farmstands follows.

Frederick Alvin "Allie" Briggs opened Allie's Hand-Cut Do-nut Shop in North Kingstown, Rhode Island, in 1968. By the end of his first day, Briggs had sold nearly one hundred dozen doughnuts at thirty-nine cents per dozen. Nearly two decades later, Allie's Donuts was selling four hundred dozen doughnuts a day in the winter months and up to eight hundred dozen a day in the summer. Some of those doughnuts ended up in Allie's signature doughnut cake—a ten-inch confection that transforms the dough for a dozen doughnuts into a personalized cake. Briggs turned the business over to his daughter and son-in-law, Anne Briggs Drescher and Walter "Bud" Drescher, in 1986. They, in turn, passed the reins to their son Matthew Drescher. But Matthew's tenure became controversial when he introduced politics into the doughnut space in 2020, and he stepped down as chief operating officer in 2021 for what he called "mostly physical and some professional reasons."

Donut Dip's distinctive neon pylon sign has been welcoming customers to this multigeneration sweet spot for more than fifty years. Charles Shields and his son Richard opened the state-of-the-art shop on busy Route 5 in West Springfield, Massachusetts, in 1957. Richard's son Paul joined the family business in the 1980s, and his daughter Katie began working behind the counter in 2013.

Richard Bowen founded Honey Dew Donuts in Mansfield, Massachusetts, in 1973. Fifty years later, he reminisced about that first store. "Back then customers would sit, have a cup of coffee, enjoy a doughnut, and talk about anything and everything," he told *Rhode Island Monthly*. "And in those early days we sold coffee and doughnuts, period. There was no flavored iced coffee or breakfast sandwiches." Today, Honey Dew (the company dropped Donuts from its name, just like Dunkin') operates a franchise model and has about 120 locations in New England.

Bob and June Kane opened their namesake doughnut shop in Saugus, Massachusetts, in 1955. Peter and Kay Delios entered the picture in the late 1980s. They had recently sold Mrs. Foster's Donuts in Lynn, which they owned from 1969 to 1986, and purchased KANE'S DONUTS in 1988. The Delioses kept the bakery's original name and worked to restore the shop's reputation, which had slipped before they took over. With a range of yeast, filled and cake doughnuts—and flavors like Crème Brûlée, Maple Bacon and Chocolate Glazed—they succeeded, and the bakery became a go-to spot. Unfortunately, when the Delioses passed on ownership to their five children, backroom squabbles became public. Paul Delios filed a lawsuit against his four siblings in 2022; as of this writing, the complaint had not been resolved.

Neil Bukowski quit his job at the age of forty and learned the doughnut business. He opened NEIL'S DONUTS in Wallingford, Connecticut, in 2001, and his son Rob runs the company's second location in Middletown. Neil's offers a mix of traditional and over-the-top doughnuts; flavors include Double Chocolate (chocolate cake doughnut dipped in chocolate icing), Samoa (raised doughnut dipped in caramel icing, topped with toasted coconut and drizzled with chocolate icing) and Blueberry Crumb (raised doughnut with blueberry filling, glazed and topped with lemon crumb).

The Hard-Pressed Cider Company in Jamestown, Rhode Island, offers fresh-made cider doughnuts. *Courtesy of author.*

Robert Swanson, owner of the HARD-PRESSED CIDER COMPANY, designed a cider trailer and started pressing cider at local orchards in 2011. In 2014, he established a permanent base at Windmist Farm in Jamestown, Rhode Island, and began making cider doughnuts the next year. His doughnuts include fresh apple pieces, fresh-pressed cider, cinnamon, nutmeg and a secret ingredient.

APPLECREST FARM is New Hampshire's oldest and largest apple orchard. Walter Baldwin Farmer planted the farm's first apple trees in 1913. The Wagner family purchased the property in 1954, and today, the fourth generation of Wagners operates the Hampton Falls farm. The farm store sells fresh fruits and vegetables, local delicacies and baked goods—including cider doughnuts.

Naturally, Maine has potato doughnuts. Leigh Kellis set about to make a healthier doughnut; her secret ingredient was potato. She opened her first brick-and-mortar store in Portland in 2012 with support from her family. The Holy Donut now has five storefronts in Maine and is still family owned. The cake-style doughnut offerings include maple, toasted coconut, old-fashioned, dark chocolate sea salt and maple bacon; vegan, gluten-free and seasonal options like sweet potato ginger are also available.

The Chichester Country Store in Chichester, New Hampshire, can trace its history to Caleb Pearson. A veteran of the Revolutionary War, Pearson settled in Chichester, where he built a grain mill and opened a tavern. Over the next two hundred years, the tavern was moved, expanded, transformed into an inn, renamed and sold multiple times. Today, the Chichester Country Store, officially established in 1847, sells sandwiches, beverages and—especially—cider doughnuts.

Cider Bellies Doughnuts are a seasonal treat at Moulton Farm in Meredith, New Hampshire. The farm has been around since the 1890s; the doughnut stand opened in 2011. Jessica Stephens founded the business, inspired by cider doughnut stands in her native Upstate New York. In addition to the traditional sugar toppings, Cider Bellies offers maple, chocolate and lemon drizzle.

Benjamin Franklin Clyde established a cider mill in Mystic, Connecticut, in 1881. After a few years of processing apples at local mills, Clyde purchased his own equipment in 1898. He installed a steam-operated cider press, which is still in use. A piece of living history, B.F. Clyde's Cider Mill has been designated a National Historic Landmark and a National Mechanical Engineering Site. Today, fourth-, fifth- and sixth-generation members of the Clyde family are producing the company's signature cider doughnuts, sweet and hard cider and apple wine.

Cold Hollow Cider Mill has been making apple cider and doughnuts in Waterbury Center, Vermont, since 1974. The company uses a vintage rack-and-cloth press to produce its cider and makes cider doughnuts year round.

In 1955, Dot (known as Nana) Congdon and her son-in-law Herb Brooks built Congdon's Doughnuts on U.S. Route 1 in Wells, Maine. Herb and his wife, Bev, expanded their business over the next few years, adding doughnut shops in Old Orchard Beach, Kennebunk and Ogunquit. Herb's sister

Eleanor and her husband, Richard Leech, took over the business when Herb and Bev were killed in an airplane crash in 1965. Congdon's offers an array of raised, filled, chocolate and plain doughnuts—even doggy doughnuts—along with Maine treats like whoopie pies. In 2017, Congdon's added a food truck park for evening dining called Congdon's After Dark.

Red Apple Farm was founded in Phillipston, Massachusetts, in 1912. Carolyn and A. Spaulding Rose purchased the farm in 1929, and the property is still in the family. The farm grows eleven kinds of McIntosh apples and is home to a century-old McIntosh tree that still produces fruit. Cider doughnuts are available at the farm store and at the Boston Public Market, where a doughnut assembly line is front and center.

Stone Mountain Farm in Belmont, New Hampshire, started as a dairy farm. The Rolfe family purchased the property in 1963 after its dairy days were over; Joseph and Cindy Rolfe bought the land in 2009 and turned it into a high-density apple orchard. In addition to cider doughnuts, Stone Mountain Farm blends two iconic New England treats with its whoopie pie doughnut—two cider doughnuts connected by a generous blob of frosting.

Twin Donuts opened in Boston's Allston neighborhood in the 1950s. Accounts vary, but the shop was likely named after the twin sons born to the owner of the nearby Model Café in 1953. A local landmark—known both for its doughnuts and its roof-mounted pink neon sign—the shop closed in 2025.

Doughboys

Fried dough—that staple of boardwalks, county fairs and amusement parks—has many names. People call these treats beaver tails, elephant ears and fried bread. Rhode Islanders call them doughboys.

With locations in Warwick and Narragansett, Iggy's is the best-known purveyor of these fried confections. Iggy's doughboys are small squares of fried dough, sold hot and available plain or dusted with sugar (powdered, granulated or cinnamon).

But the doughboy story began before Iggy's, when Frieda and George "Gus" Gionis opened a hamburger stand in the Oakland Beach section of Warwick in 1924. The couple added Mrs. Gus's Restaurant in 1934 and a takeout stand in 1940 called Gus's on the Bay, which sold doughboys and other boardwalk treats. Frieda took over when Gus died in 1956, with the

An assortment of doughboys from Iggy's in Narragansett, Rhode Island. *Courtesy of author.*

help of her brother John Rengigas. Not only does the Gionis family claim to have invented the name *doughboy* ("25 years before Pillsbury named their chubby little dough figure," the Mrs. Gus's website boasts), but they estimate they sold some twenty million doughboys between 1940 and 1985, when the restaurant closed.

The family sold the business in 1986, and the new owner leased the eatery to Sally and Gaetano "Guy" Gravino in 1989. They renamed it Iggy's. Their children David Gravino and MaryAnn Soares purchased Iggy's in 1999 and still run the place.

Where did the name Iggy's come from? Oddly enough, Guy Gravino got his nickname from a license plate. When his children were young, his license plate was IG-6. The kids started calling their dad "IG," which evolved into Iggy, and the name stuck.

CANNOLI WARS

"Leave the gun. Take the cannoli," is one of the most memorable lines from *The Godfather* and enshrined the pastry in popular culture and film history. Cannoli are tube-shaped deep-fried pastry shells with a sweet filling of ricotta cheese. (*Cannolo*, the singular form of the word, means "little tube" in Italian.)

Cannoli originated in Sicily, possibly as a fertility symbol, but bakeries in Boston's North End (the city's version of Little Italy) have turned them into an art form. Three of the city's best-known cannoli bakeries are Modern Pastry Shop, Mike's Pastry and Bova's Bakery—all within walking distance of one another—and everyone has a favorite.

Modern Pastry opened on Hanover Street in 1930 and has remained in the Picariello family ever since. Also on Hanover Street, Michael Mercogliano started Mike's Pastry in 1946, and today his stepson Angelo Papa keeps the tradition going. Bova's is located on nearby Salem Street, where Antonio Bova started his own bakery in 1926. Today, the family-owned shop is open 24/7 and offers everything from tiramisu to cannoli. But which cannolo is best? Each bakery has fierce defenders, and it all comes down to a matter of taste.

Did you know? Boston-based Harpoon Brewery makes a flavor called Mike's Pastry Cannoli Stout. The beermaker and bakery developed a brew that combines cannoli shells, cocoa nibs, lactose and vanilla to re-create the flavor of the classic treat. Not to be outdone, Lord Hobo Brewing Company collaborated with Modern Pastry to release its Tiramisu Stout.

ZEPPOLE

A *zeppola* is an Italian sweet that consists of a fried ring of choux pastry, usually filled with pastry cream and topped with powdered sugar and a maraschino cherry. *Zeppole* (the plural form) resemble glammed-up eclairs or cream puffs, and many food historians trace their origins to Pasquale Pintauro, a renowned pastry chef in nineteenth-century Naples. (He is also credited with popularizing the sfogliatella pastry.)

Zeppole are a big deal in Rhode Island. The treat is associated with St. Joseph's Day, which is March 19, and the Ocean State has turned the pastry into a delicious tradition. Every spring, Rhode Island's many Italian bakeries pull out all the stops. Some shops stick with the traditional recipe, but others add their own touches like chocolate or strawberry filling. A few even add Irish cream flavoring or green-tinted pistachios to the filling in a nod to St. Patrick's Day, celebrated just two days before.

For most establishments, zeppole are a seasonal treat, sold exclusively in the weeks surrounding St. Joseph's Day, but others offer them year round. Either way, the days leading up to the feast day can be intense, and some bakeries prepare thousands of pastries to meet the spring demand.

Chapter 7

FROZEN

Fribbles, Frappes, Creemees and Cabinets

New Englanders love ice cream. Even in the dead of winter, when common sense suggests hunkering down with a mug of hot chocolate, they choose ice cream. A widely reported statistic said that New Englanders consume an average of 22.8 quarts of ice cream per person per year, compared to the national average of 15.1 quarts. That number from the International Ice Cream Association dates from 1987 and has not been updated. And yet, it still feels true. Maybe the real question is not how much ice cream do New Englanders eat, but why? One answer is the sheer variety of ice cream purveyors in the region, some of which are profiled here.

BAILEY'S

Bostonians of a certain age remember Bailey's. The small Massachusetts chain sold candy, sandwiches and—most memorably—ice cream sundaes dripping with hot fudge sauce.

Bailey's was special. As the *Boston Globe* wrote in 2007, "For more than 100 years, Bailey's on West Street served hand-made chocolates, gooey hot fudge sundaes, and chopped ham-and-sweet-pickle sandwiches to customers who sat at marble-topped tables." The sundaes were served in silver tulip-shaped bowls presented on a silver saucer that caught the overflowing fudge or butterscotch sauce.

John B. Bailey and Dudley H. Page started a confectionery on West Street in downtown Boston in 1873. Originally called Bailey and Page (or possibly Page and Bailey), the business started as a candy shop; the ice cream came later. Bailey bought out his partner in 1876, and Page went on to start the candy company Page and Shaw with Charles N. Shaw.

In 1900, Bailey sold the shop to his bookkeeper Sally Dow for $18,000. Dow, who was later known as Sarah Dow Gilman, is said to be responsible for Bailey's signature overflowing sundaes. Starting under her leadership, Bailey's sent chocolates to every U.S. president from Theodore Roosevelt to John F. Kennedy—Calvin Coolidge was said to enjoy the fudge balls dipped in fondant—and she also kept track of the favorites of Bailey's non-presidential customers.

After Dow died 1943, her husband, Osmon (sometimes Osman) B. Gilman, continued to run the shop. Franklin Wyman Jr. purchased the West Street location in 1960 and added ten cafés in Greater Boston. In 1983, Wyman sold the chain to Frank Benson, who was the former president of Fanny Farmer Candies. Joey Crugnale, who had previously purchased Steve's Ice Cream in Somerville, bought Bailey's in 1987.

Crugnale had big ideas for updating Bailey's when he bought the chain. "I think it will be a 100-store chain throughout New England in seven or eight years," he told the *Boston Globe*. "But we will be very careful with the site selections." First, he said, the chopped ham-and-pickle sandwiches had to go. His customers were not happy about the change. "I probably got 50 calls from little old ladies who have been going to Bailey's for 50 years who were really up in arms when I said I was going to take the chopped ham and pickle sandwiches off the menu," he said. "But there's just no future in ham and pickles."

Crugnale initially pumped money into the business, opening two new locations and renovating some of the existing stores. But after changing the menu, Bailey's lost many of its long-term customers and could not compete with new lunch spots popping up in downtown Boston. The ice cream scene had changed as well, and customers were flocking to scoop shops with super-premium ice cream and funky décor. Crugnale eventually sold the Bailey's name, two locations and the hot fudge recipe to Michael Mazzaferro, who also owned Connelly's Candies. Asked what happened, Crugnale told the *Globe*, "It's not one of my prouder moments. There's really not much to talk about."

BRIGHAM'S

In 1914, the Symmes brothers opened an ice cream and candy shop in Boston's Post Office Square called the Durand Company. Ten years later, Edward L. Brigham opened the Little Shop, an ice cream parlor outside the city in Newton Highlands. The two businesses merged in 1929, opened three more stores and an ice cream manufacturing plant and established the foundation for a business that would keep going for almost a century.

Brigham's made it through the Depression years, keeping its employees and accepting IOUs from customers. As economic conditions improved, the business added twenty new stores. In 1940, Brigham's added baked goods to its menu with the acquisition of Dorothy Muriel's bakery. The Durand Company moved to Cambridge and continued making chocolates until the early 1960s.

Under new corporate ownership, Brigham's added more locations; the chain peaked at about one hundred shops in the 1970s. But things began to go downhill in the 1980s, and Brigham's was in tough shape by the start of the twenty-first century.

Facing competition from premium ice cream brands like Ben & Jerry's, the company tried to expand its offerings while emphasizing its Boston roots. In 2003, Brigham's held a contest to name a new flavor to commemorate its upcoming ninetieth anniversary. The winning entry was Reverse the Curse—vanilla with chocolate-covered peanuts, caramel cups and fudge swirls—which referred to the so-called Curse of the Bambino. At the time, the Boston Red Sox had not won a World Series since 1918, and the legend blamed the winless streak on the sale of Babe Ruth from the Red Sox to the New York Yankees in 1919. Brigham's launched the flavor at the beginning of the 2004 Major League Baseball season, and Reverse the Curse became the best-selling new flavor in Brigham's history. And then something unexpected happened: the Red Sox won the World Series. The curse was reversed. Brigham's pivoted and introduced Curse Reversed to celebrate the team's victory. Brigham's tried to recapture the magic in 2006 with Fluffernutter ice cream, which was based on the peanut butter and Marshmallow Fluff sandwich of the same name.

But the new flavors could not halt Brigham's falling fortunes, and the company's days were numbered. Brigham's was split up in 2008. H.P. Hood bought the ice cream brand name and still makes ice cream under the Brigham's name. Deal Metrics bought the restaurants and closed the thirteen company-owned stores after filing for bankruptcy in 2009. The franchisees survived for a few more years, but all were gone by 2013.

FRIENDLY'S

In 1935, brothers Curtis and S. Prestley Blake, age eighteen and twenty, respectively, borrowed $547 from their parents and opened a shop in Springfield, Massachusetts, called Friendly Ice Cream. The brothers charged a nickel for two scoops of ice cream, which was half the price of other ice cream establishments, and the shop was an immediate success.

A second Friendly opened in 1940, this time in West Springfield. After a hiatus during World War II, Friendly reopened in 1945 and began to expand. By 1951, there were ten Friendly shops in western Massachusetts and Connecticut. The company entered the metropolitan Boston market in 1959 with a shop in Dedham, and Friendly moved to its new headquarters in Wilbraham, Massachusetts, the next year. A creamery next door made ice cream for all Friendly locations.

As its name suggested, Friendly was a "family-friendly place serving feel-good ice cream treats," as the *Boston Globe* wrote in 2007. "It quickly became a hangout for youths after school, ballgames, and concerts." The menu featured items with quirky names: Fribble (a thick ice cream shake once known as the Awful Awful), Fishamajig (a fried fish sandwich with melted cheese and tartar sauce) and Jim Dandy (a banana split).

By 1974, Friendly had five hundred restaurants in the Northeast and Mid-Atlantic, and the brothers began to disagree about the direction of the company. Instead of working out their differences, the Blakes sold the Friendly chain to the Hershey Company in 1979 for about $164 million. Under Hershey's ownership, Friendly grew to eight hundred stores, and the shops added products to their sundaes from Hershey offerings like Reese's Pieces and Heath Bar Crunch.

But faced with increasing competition and high labor costs, Hershey sold Friendly to fast-food executive Donald Smith and a group of investors for about $375 million in 1988; that is when Friendly Ice Cream became Friendly's. Many analysts believed Smith paid too much for the struggling restaurant chain, and the new owners borrowed heavily to close the deal. They began shutting down restaurants to pay off their debt.

Prestley Blake was watching the troubles of his former company from the sidelines and reentered the fray in 2000. Friendly's had gone public in 1997, and Blake bought about $2 million worth of company stock. His 12 percent stake made him Friendly's largest shareholder. "I did it to get some attention," he told the *New York Times*. "When you become a major stockholder, that gets you attention pretty fast."

Did you know? In 2014, Prestley Blake built a replica of Thomas Jefferson's home Monticello next to his residence in Somers, Connecticut, and donated it to Hillsdale College. No one knew what inspired the project. "Dad gets this idea that he wants to build Monticello, and we all go, 'Oh my god, that's such a weird idea,'" his stepdaughter Susan Abello told the *Hillsdale Collegian* in 2023. "I admit I don't have the vision, but Pres had the vision and he loved that building."

In 2003, Blake filed a lawsuit against Friendly's accusing Smith of misusing company funds; he seemed particularly outraged by Smith's use of the Friendly's corporate jet. Smith eventually reimbursed the company for some jet travel but did not acknowledge any other wrongdoing. Curtis Blake believed his brother's actions were hurting the company, and the brothers had a falling out. "My brother forgot we sold the company," Curtis told the *Boston Globe*. "He used to call Hershey's regularly and with Smith he did the same thing. My brother never wanted to let go."

Friendly's never got back on track, although the brothers eventually reconciled. Sun Capital Partners took the company private in 2007 for about $340 million. Two bankruptcy filings followed in 2011 and 2020; Amici Partners Group acquired Friendly's in 2021 and is trying to revive the brand, mostly through franchising. In March 2024, Friendly's had just 103 locations, and 2 more were slated for closure.

Curtis died in 2019 at the age of 102, and Prestley passed away 2 years later at 106.

HOULTON FARMS DAIRY BAR

Mike Clark started Houlton Farms Dairy in 1938 on land that was once a baseball field. Located in Houlton, Maine, the dairy was the first facility in Aroostook County to pasteurize its milk, and milkmen delivered the company's products to local households until 1974.

Clark sold the business to longtime employee Milton Lambert Jr. in 1977. Lambert sold the business in 1981 to Alice and Leonard Lincoln. Alice had been working at the dairy as a bookkeeper since 1965; her son Eric started working in the summers when he was just sixteen. Today, the Lincoln family—Alice, Leonard and sons Eric and Jim—still owns the company.

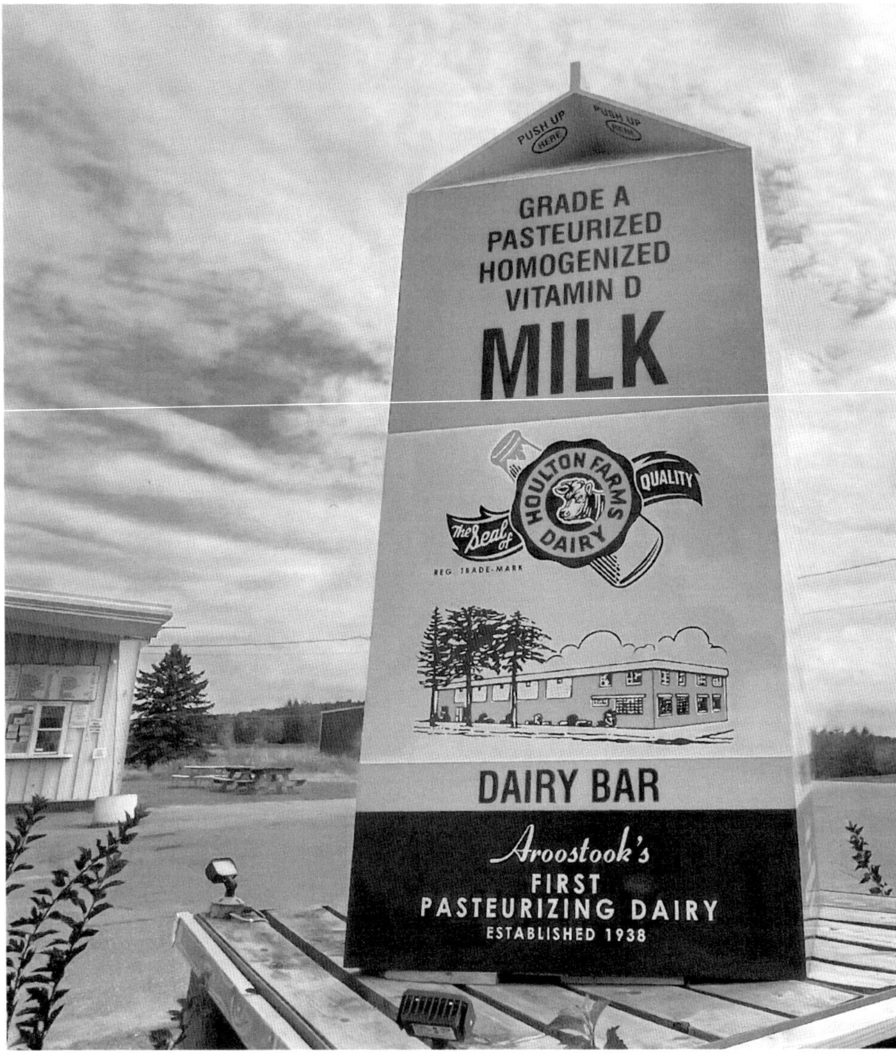

The giant milk carton at Houlton Farms Dairy Bar in Presque Isle, Maine. *Courtesy of author.*

The dairy expanded in 1983 with an ice cream bar in Presque Isle and its larger-than-life milk carton along U.S. Route 1. Two others followed in Caribou (1987) and Houlton (1988). The stands started with just seven flavors, but today there are dozens, including maple walnut, Almond Joy, Grape-Nut, cookie dough and bubble gum. In 2024, the company announced its decision to stop producing milk and to focus on ice cream, butter and lemonade.

GIFFORD'S ICE CREAM

Gifford's Ice Cream is a fifth-generation family-owned company based in Skowhegan, Maine. The company traces its roots to the late 1800s, when Nathaniel Main had a milk and ice cream business in Pawcatuck, Connecticut. Nathaniel's son Chester joined the business in 1915. Fast-forward to 1947, when Chester's daughter Audrey married Randall Gifford. The couple and their four children moved to Randall's home state of Maine in the 1970s and purchased dairies in Skowhegan and Farmington.

In the 1980s, Gifford's opened ice cream stands in Skowhegan, Farmington, Bangor and Waterville. The company sold its milk business in 1983 to Oakhurst Dairy so that sons Roger and John could focus on the ice cream side of the business. The brothers still own the company, and the next generation of Giffords is running the day-to-day operations.

Gifford's sources its milk and cream from local family farms and makes 90 percent of its flavorings from scratch. The company's one hundred flavors of ice cream and frozen treats include some Maine-inspired offerings (Fly Fishing Fudge and Maine Black Bear) and a few fanciful combinations (Spicy Strawberry Pretzel and I Scream for Cake). Gifford's has also partnered with New England professional sports teams to produce special flavors: Dough Your Job (New England Patriots), Full Quart Pretz (Boston Celtics), Power Play Fudge (Boston Bruins) and Sea Dogs Biscuit (Portland Sea Dogs). And in 2012, L.L. Bean asked Gifford's to create Muddy Bean Boots, a limited-edition ice cream to celebrate the retailer's 100th anniversary.

In 2011, Gifford's Ice Cream purchased Gifford's Ice Cream and Candy, a troubled—and unrelated—ice cream chain based in Maryland.

HOWARD JOHNSON'S

Howard Deering Johnson opened his first soda fountain in Quincy, Massachusetts, in 1925. Encouraged by the success of his inaugural venture, Johnson opened three seasonal ice cream stands in 1926–27 and a full-service restaurant in 1929. Johnson began franchising in 1935 with a restaurant in Orleans, a town on Cape Cod, and more followed quickly. By the end of 1940, Howard Johnson's was a full-fledged chain, with 132 restaurants, a mix of franchises and company-owned restaurants.

With the growth of automobile travel, Howard Johnson's sought to attract motorists by locating restaurants at busy intersections and highly visible sites. (Hilltops were ideal.) The bright orange roofs, topped with a steeple and a weathervane, essentially served as billboards for the restaurants. The twenty-eight flavors of ice cream and kid-friendly menus appealed to families on the move.

Howard Johnson's was the largest restaurant chain in America by the mid-1960s, and the company was riding high. Howard D. Johnson retired in 1968 and turned the company over to his son Howard B. Johnson, known as "Bud." Bud Johnson continued to expand the company, and Howard Johnson's had more than one thousand restaurants (company-owned and franchised) in 1979.

But times were changing. The company started to cut costs, quality control was relaxed and customers began to perceive the chain as old-fashioned. Bud Johnson sold Howard Johnson's in 1979, and the company continued to decline. The last Howard Johnson's restaurant closed in Lake George, New York, in 2022, almost one hundred years after Howard Deering Johnson began scooping ice cream in Massachusetts.

H.P. HOOD

Vermont native Harvey Perley Hood started a milk delivery service in Charlestown, Massachusetts, in 1846. Ten years later, he bought a farm in Derry, New Hampshire, to expand into the wholesale dairy business. Harvey Hood's three sons—Charles, Gilbert and Edward—took over the business after their father passed away in 1900. By then, the company had incorporated as H.P. Hood and Sons.

H.P. Hood had a series of firsts during its years of business: first New England dairy to pasteurize milk, first to package milk in glass bottles and first to transport its products by rail. Advertisements appearing in the *Boston Globe* in 1912 touted the advantages of Hood's pasteurized milk. "Authorities have stated that thousands of people have been made sick in Greater Boston in the last few years from using unsafe milk," the ad began. After extolling the benefits of Hood's "Perfect Pasteurization" process, the ad concluded with the tagline "It costs no more than unsafe milk."

In 1929, the company celebrated the opening of its new bottling and pasteurizing facility in Charlestown with great fanfare. Nearly three hundred

The smokestack from the H.P. Hood factory in Charlestown, Massachusetts. *Courtesy of author.*

industry representatives, health officials and local dignitaries attended a gala dinner; press reports said the guests cheered as company president Dr. Charles H. Hood sliced into an ice cream replica of the new factory. Some seventy years after Harvey P. Hood bought that farm in New Hampshire, his company was sourcing milk from six thousand farmers. The factory has since been converted into a mixed-use campus, but the original smokestack remains as a reminder of the city's industrial past.

Agway, a farmers' cooperative based in Upstate New York, acquired H.P. Hood in 1980, ending generations of Massachusetts ownership. The Kaneb family purchased Hood in 1995, when it was losing market share, and still owns the company. "This returns Hood to New England ownership, and we're going to try to go back to Hood's strengths—of being Hood," said John A. Kaneb at the time of the sale.

Many New Englanders associate Hood with Hoodsie Cups. Introduced in 1947 and still available, Hoodsies are three-ounce paper cups of ice cream, evenly divided between chocolate and vanilla, and served with a small wooden spoon. "For many of us, Hoodsie Cups (or just plain 'Hoodsies') are a tastebud-reminder of childhood, when the cups were often handed out at birthday and classroom parties, summer cookouts, and church suppers," Aimee Tucker wrote on NewEngland.com. "We remember pulling up on the little tab that peeled back the paper lid to reveal the ice cream below, and gleefully digging in with the accompanying wooden spoon, which was really just the shortened, hourglass-shaped equivalent of a tongue depressor." Hoodsie Cups are such a local tradition that the Boston Police Department teamed up with Hood to launch Operation Hoodsie as part of its community policing activities. Since 2010, police officers have traveled around the city in an ice cream truck to hand out Hoodsie Cups to neighborhood residents.

Also cementing Hood's connection with Boston, a giant Hood-branded milk bottle has served as an ice cream stand in front of the Boston Children's Museum since 1977. The bottle started south of the city in Taunton, Massachusetts, where ice cream vendor Arthur Gagner built the structure in 1934. An example of roadside pop architecture—where buildings took the form of animals or products like doughnuts or hot dogs—the wooden milk bottle stood forty feet tall. After the bottle was abandoned in 1967, Hood purchased the deteriorating structure, restored it and donated it to the museum.

NEWPORT CREAMERY

Newport Creamery is an ice cream and casual restaurant chain in Rhode Island and southeastern Massachusetts. The company traces its roots to 1928, when Samuel Rector and two partners took over a wholesale dairy in Newport, Rhode Island. Rector became the sole owner in 1933.

Rector and his son Mason (who had joined his father in 1932) entered the ice cream business in 1940, when they opened a milk bar called Newport Creamery in Middletown, Rhode Island. After selling their dairy business in 1948, they opened a second restaurant in Pawtucket. A Providence location, launched in 1953, was the first Newport Creamery restaurant to offer food in addition to ice cream. But the cafés were mostly associated with a thick ice cream shake dubbed the Awful Awful.

Newport Creamery expanded throughout Rhode Island during the 1950s and 1960s; the chain had three hundred employees and thirteen locations in the state when Mason Rector died in 1966. (Samuel had passed away in 1957.) In 1999, the Rector family, which still owned Newport Creamery, sold the company to Florida businessman Robert Swain for $7.6 million. Swain tried to expand the chain into Massachusetts and Connecticut, but his efforts were unsuccessful. Newport Creamery filed for bankruptcy in 2000 and was purchased by Jan Companies for $1.55 million in 2001. Newport Creamery—still owned and operated by the Jan Companies—had eight locations in Rhode Island and two in Massachusetts at the end of 2024.

The original Newport Creamery in Middletown, Rhode Island. *Courtesy of author.*

CABINETS

A coffee cabinet at Delekta's in Warren, Rhode Island. *Courtesy of author.*

A frozen confection with a distinctive name, a coffee cabinet is a Rhode Island tradition. The drink has three ingredients—coffee ice cream, coffee syrup and milk—and is known as a frappe in Massachusetts and a milkshake almost everywhere else.

Cabinets have been around for over a century, but no one knows for sure where the curious name came from. *The Dictionary of American Regional English* traced the earliest printed reference to a *coffee cabinet* to a 1903 publication called *Spatula*, which described a drink made with coffee syrup, eggs, cream, ice cream and shaved ice. A popular claim says the name referred to the wooden cabinet where soda fountain workers stored their blender. A related theory traces the name to a different kind of kitchen cabinet. In 1929, Frigidaire introduced the first home freezer, which was called the "Ice Cream Cabinet," although the innovation came more than twenty years after the *Spatula* reference. Another theory suggested the name is a Rhode Island–accented corruption of "carbonated." And mixologists theorized that the drink drew its name from the Royal Cabinet cocktail, an orange-flavored creamy cocktail popular in Chicago in the 1890s.

Did you know? In most parts of the United States, a milkshake is a blend of ice cream, syrup and milk. In New England, especially Massachusetts, that combination is called a frappe. (The *e* is silent.) In Rhode Island, a frappe is called a cabinet. For traditionalists in the land of frappes and cabinets, a milkshake consists of milk plus syrup whipped until it is foamy.

Delekta Pharmacy has been serving coffee cabinets for decades. The creamy treats are often touted as the best in Rhode Island, and Delekta uses house-made coffee syrup along with the requisite coffee ice cream and milk. The pharmacy has been on Main Street in Warren, Rhode Island, since the 1850s, when it was owned by William Bennett. Bennett sold the pharmacy, then known as Bennett's, to his business partner, Howard DeWolf, in 1921. Ignatius Delekta began working at the pharmacy in 1926; he purchased the shop in 1944 and renamed it Delekta Pharmacy. Delekta retired in 1971, and his children Ignatius Delekta Jr. and Kathleen Delekta Lowney took over. In 2017, Delekta Pharmacy transformed into Delekta's Corner Store to focus on its soda fountain offerings, including cabinets; the pharmacy side of the business closed.

AWFUL AWFUL

The story of the Awful Awful spans three states, several decades and at least one bankruptcy.

In the 1940s, a New Jersey ice cream shop called Bond's developed a creamy drink that mixed ice milk with flavored syrups. A customer supposedly called the drink "awful big and awful good," and the name stuck. Bond's shared its Awful Awful recipe in 1958:

Awful Awful

Pour 6 ounces of milk into an Awful Awful glass or paper cup.
Add 2 ounces of flavored syrup as specified by customer.
Scoop in 3 dips of ice cream.
Place glass or cup on mixer and whip 'til ice cream is incorporated.
Serve with straw of jumbo diameter.

Three things jump out from that recipe. First, apart from the branding, this could be a recipe for any milkshake, frappe or cabinet (depending on local terminology). Second, the so-called ice milk is not a special formulation; it is ice cream plus milk. And, finally, that jumbo straw is key to enjoying the thick drink.

The recipe may have been generic, but the name was anything but. Bond's trademarked the Awful Awful name in 1948 and soon licensed it to two New England businesses: Newport Creamery and Friendly. The deal had one key proviso: neither eatery could use the Awful Awful name in New Jersey.

By the 1960s, Friendly wanted to expand into New Jersey and held a contest to rename its signature ice cream drink. Three people received $100 each for suggesting the winning name: Fribble. When Bond's went bankrupt in 1970, Newport Creamery scooped up the Awful Awful trademark for $1,000 and sells the drink with the double name today. Friendly's has changed its formula for the Fribble several times but still offers the sweet concoction.

CREEMEES

Creemees are Vermont's answer to soft-serve ice cream. But while the frozen treats come out of a soft-serve machine, they have more butterfat and less air than the conventional product.

The treat is a sure sign of summer in Vermont and is beloved by locals and tourists alike. "Every year, when winter gives way to fool's spring, then second winter, then mud season, and then finally spring, creemee purveyors put out their sandwich boards and flip their signs to 'open,'" Tanner Bowden wrote for the Eater website. "Vermonters adjust their routines to include frequent visits to ice cream shops, lining up in front of takeout windows."

No one knows exactly where the name *creemee* came from. Neither is there an accepted spelling, although two pairs of *E*s are the most common. Some think the word simply describes the treat's creamy texture. Others suspect that creemee is a corruption of *crème glacée*, the term for ice cream in neighboring Quebec.

Maple is the traditional creemee flavor, but vanilla, chocolate and black raspberry are widely available. (A "twist" is a cone or cup with two flavors swirled together.) Some trace the maple flavor to the 1981 Vermont State Fair in Rutland, but others are not so sure. Regardless of the origins, the maple creemee is a happy blend of the state's two defining elements: maple syrup production and dairy farming.

Creemees are widely available across Vermont and can be found in ice cream parlors, roadside shacks, gas stations, restaurants and maple syrup houses. Every creemee is different, and everyone has a favorite. Here are just a few of Vermont's hundreds of creemee purveyors.

Top: Roadside creemee sign in Vermont. *Courtesy of author.*

Bottom: Ice cream cone sign outside lu·lu Ice Cream in Vergennes, Vermont. *Courtesy of author.*

The Dairy Creme in Montpelier is a converted A&W stand. The structure was relocated from Middlesex to its current location on U.S. Route 2 when Interstate 89 was constructed in 1960. The shop owners acquired two 1950s-era machines from "a well-known international soft serve chain," and Dairy Creme was open for business.

Cliff and Laurie Dodge purchased the roadside stand in 1997 and gradually expanded its offerings with food options and additional creemee flavors. In an only-in-Vermont twist, Cliff began selling wood pellets from the Dairy Creme, which allowed the Dodges to operate the family business year round. "It has been a family-operated business since day one," Cliff said. "We've each taken turns at all of the different roles, and two of my three grandchildren have worked here." The Dodges sold the Dairy Creme in 2024.

Laura Mack opened an ice cream shop she called lu•lu in Bristol in 2014. Four years later, the shop moved to its current location in Vergennes, which is Vermont's smallest city. lu•lu specializes in what it calls "farm-to-spoon" ice cream. The store makes all its ice cream from scratch in small batches and uses no preservatives or mixes; even the sprinkles are colored with fruit and vegetable extracts.

The Canteen Creemee Company in Waitsfield has fun with its creemees. Besides selling traditional flavors like maple and chocolate, the shop offers exotic combinations like the mega-maple Bad Larry, which is a maple creemee with maple crystal, maple drizzle, maple cookie and maple floss, or the decadent Special Brownie, which is a chocolate creemee accented with brownies, caramel, whipped cream and chocolate dip.

A cheery yellow sign welcomed customers to the Village Creeme Stand in Bristol. Tom and Claire Wallace opened the spot in 1982, and their children and grandchildren worked in the business until Tom passed away in 2023. The family did not open for the 2024 season, and the creemee spot has not announced its next steps as of this writing.

Scoops, with stores in Woodstock, Vermont, and Hanover, New Hampshire, sells what they call "farm-to-cone" ice cream. The creemees use maple syrup from Bourdon Maple Farm, and the hard-serve ice cream comes from two Vermont companies: Mountain Creamery and Wilcox.

JIMMIES

Confectionery sprinkles are small pieces of candy used to add color, texture and a touch of whimsy to desserts. The most common types are multicolored sprinkles (sometimes called "rainbow") and chocolate sprinkles. Sprinkles go by many names, including the evocative "hundreds and thousands" in England. But in New England and Philadelphia, sprinkles are often called "jimmies," especially the chocolate variety.

No one really knows where the word *jimmies* came from—the first known appearance in print was in 1947—but theories about the word's origins abound. Some see a connection to the early term *jim-jam*, which was first used in sixteenth-century English to refer to something trivial like a knickknack or gimcrack.

A popular theory within the confectionery industry traces the origin of jimmies to a Brooklyn candy maker. Sam Born founded the Just Born company in 1923. Known today for Peeps, Mike and Ike and Hot Tamales, the company credits founder Born with multiple inventions, including the Born Sucker Machine (which inserted sticks into lollipops) and the technology to make chocolate sprinkles.

Just Born began making chocolate sprinkles around 1930 and apparently came up with the name. A company spokeswoman offered the following explanation:

> *Jimmies were our registered trademark up into the mid-1960s, and we have items in our archives from that time with the word "Jimmies" and the Just Born logo on them. According to former Just Born CEO Ross Born, Jimmies received their unique name from the associate who ran the machine that made them: Jimmy Bartholomew. Jimmy started at Just Born in 1930.*

But Bostonians often attribute the name *jimmies* to a well-known New England charity cause. In 1947, the Brigham's ice cream chain began offering jimmies free of charge on ice cream cones and dishes. In 1948, the Variety Children's Charity of New England and the Boston Braves baseball team raised funds for a young cancer patient nicknamed Jimmy. The outreach effort was so successful that the Jimmy Fund was created that year to support the Dana Farber Cancer Institute. As for the ice cream connection, Brigham's was said to begin charging for sprinkles and donating the proceeds to the Jimmy Fund. Though the story is appealing, it appears to be apocryphal. The timeline simply does not work. With its 1948 start, the Jimmy Fund began well after jimmies acquired their name.

Because many New Englanders distinguished between chocolate jimmies and rainbow sprinkles, a troubling theory gained traction around 1997. People believed that jimmies were racist. Proponents of this theory claim that the name *jimmies* refers to Jim Crow, the segregationist laws in the American South. The fact-checking website Snopes.com called the claim unproven but equivocated a bit: "It's difficult to definitively disprove the claim because the term's entry into the English language is downright murky." Author David Wilton was more definitive. He described jimmies as "another innocent term that has been associated with false racist origins." He concluded: "All we have to prove a racial origin for jimmy is the use of jim, and the fact that some sprinkles are chocolate. Some better evidence must be presented before one can assume a racial origin for the term."

Murky origins aside, at least one ice cream purveyor took no chances. H.P. Hood, which acquired Brigham's ice cream in 2008, changed the name of its Just Jimmies flavor to Just Sprinkles around 2020.

Chapter 8

REINVENTING ICE CREAM

When Less (Air) Is More

In the late 1970s and early 1980s, New England was the center of an ice cream renaissance. Steve Herrell, Ben Cohen, Jerry Greenfield, Gus Rancatore and a few others—most of whom had no confectionery experience—changed the way people thought about ice cream. Long before observers began using the term *disruption innovation*, these pioneers upended the ice cream status quo.

FIRST STEVE'S, THEN HERRELL'S

In 1973, twenty-nine-year-old Steve Herrell began a revolution in a storefront on Elm Street in Somerville, Massachusetts, near the border with Cambridge. Herrell transformed the former dry cleaning establishment into an ice cream shop furnished with an eclectic and colorful mix of mismatched chairs and tables, a refurbished player piano and—most important—a five-gallon ice-and-salt ice cream maker from the White Mountain Freezer Company, then located in Winchendon, Massachusetts.

Steve's Ice Cream opened on June 29, 1973, and was an immediate success. Herrell wrote in his memoir *Ice Cream and Me*: "Just in the first week happy folks of all ages were streaming in and waiting in ever-larger lines each night."

Patrons queued up outside Steve's Ice Cream shop in Somerville, Massachusetts. *Courtesy of Judy Herrell.*

What made Steve's so special? The hippie-inspired décor was appealing, the flavors were innovative, the hot fudge was intensely chocolatey and the whipped cream was made from scratch. But two things defined Steve's from the beginning: the quality of the ice cream and the novelty of the mix-ins.

Steve's served rich, creamy, small-batch ice cream. One of the secrets to the creaminess was the low volume of air in the product. In its simplest form, ice cream consists of cream plus sugar and flavorings frozen into a solid state through motion or agitation. Agitation incorporates air into the mixture during the freezing process using a moving blade called a dasher. The speed of the dasher controls the amount of air in the finished product. Slower revolutions introduce less air, which creates denser ice cream (known in the industry as *low overrun*). In the 1970s, many commercial manufacturers produced ice cream with a high proportion of air in the final product (called *high overrun*). Low-overrun ice cream is heavier and creamier than the high-overrun varieties; the latter are lighter and fluffier. Consumer preferences vary, but Herrell did not equivocate. "Would you rather be eating air or ice cream?" he asked rhetorically in his memoir. To offer his signature ice cream, Herrell modified his White Mountain freezer with an engine to churn the ice cream slowly enough to create a super-premium low-overrun product.

Steve's also introduced mix-ins or, as Herrell later trademarked it, smoosh-ins. The concept was straightforward. Instead of sprinkling extras—candies, nuts or chopped-up cookies—on top of the ice cream, servers would mix the goodies into the ice cream. The result was a customized ice cream flavor, perhaps coffee ice cream with Heath bars or chocolate with Oreos. "Before I opened Steve's, to my knowledge, no ice cream anywhere contained chopped Heath bars, Reese's cups, Oreos, M&Ms, and other nationally popular candies that people know and love by name and trademark," Herrell wrote. "Once Steve's opened, the baked goods and candy industries were thereby forever married to the ice cream industry."

Although Herrell loved ice cream, he did not love running a scoop shop—especially one with lines of customers out the door every night—and he sold the business to brothers Joey and Nino Crugnale in 1977. Joey Crugnale already owned an ice cream shop called Joey's in Somerville's Teele Square and would later go on to buy the Bailey's ice cream shops and found the Bertucci's pizza chain. He sold Steve's in 1983. After a series of corporate complications, including experiments with franchising and wholesaling, Steve's closed in the late 1990s.

In the meantime, Herrell had become a piano tuner and moved to Northampton, Massachusetts. In 1980, when his noncompete clause with the Crugnales expired, Herrell decided to get back into the ice cream business. No longer allowed to use the name "Steve's Ice Cream," which he had sold along with his business, he used his last name instead.

Herrell's Homemade Ice Cream Company opened in Northampton on September 8, 1980. Herrell's followed the same model as the original Steve's: thick, creamy ice cream, interesting flavors and smoosh-ins. Herrell ran his namesake store alongside his wife (and, later, ex-wife), Judy Herrell, until he retired at the end of 2013. Today, Judy Herrell runs the Northampton shop; she added an outlet in nearby Amherst in 2024.

BEN & JERRY'S

A year after Steve Herrell sold his ice cream store, two guys from New York founded another ice cream dynasty, this time in Vermont.

Ben Cohen and Jerry Greenfield met in a seventh-grade gym class in the Long Island community of Merrick, New York. Fast-forward a few years, and the friends were weighing their career options. Cohen had dropped out of college to become a potter but had no customers. Greenfield applied to medical school but had no acceptances. So they decided to go into business together.

What led them to ice cream? "We were both fat, dumpy kids growing up and we liked to eat," Greenfield told the *Washington Post* in an interview. "So we knew we wanted to do something with food." They considered making bagels but could not afford the equipment. Instead, they plunked down five dollars for a correspondence course in ice cream making from Pennsylvania State University and aced the open-book final exam. With an investment of $12,000, they found a run-down gas station with a leaky roof in Burlington, Vermont, and turned it into an ice cream shop. Ben & Jerry's opened in 1978 with a five-gallon ice-and-salt freezer and—yes—a player piano.

Like Herrell, Cohen and Greenfield set out to make a rich and creamy product, and a lot of that came down to the speed of the dasher. But just how slowly should the dasher turn? The friends decided to conduct some research. "One of the research projects that Jerry and Ben had done on their road trips was to surreptitiously count the revolutions per minute on the ice cream freezers at other homemade scoop shops," wrote Fred "Chico" Lager in *Ben & Jerry's: The Inside Scoop*. "If twenty per minute worked for Steve's in Cambridge, they figured that twenty per minute would work for them." In a 2003 interview with the *Boston Phoenix*, Cohen and Greenfield talked about the influence of Steve Herrell on their business. "Certainly, before we started, we came and visited Steve's Ice Cream in Somerville, and we

The Ben & Jerry's Cowmobile. *Courtesy of Ben & Jerry's.*

spoke with Steve Herrell, who was really amazingly helpful for someone who didn't know us at all and had no reason to be helpful," Greenfield said. "He was just a really nice guy and very helpful, and he still makes great ice cream at Herrell's. We owe a great debt of gratitude to Steve Herrell."

Ben & Jerry's intense flavors were created out of necessity. "I've never had a very good sense of smell, and if you don't have that, you don't have a good sense of taste," Cohen told the *New York Times* in 1994. "When we began, the game was for Jerry to make a flavor I could taste with my eyes closed. To do that he had to make ice creams that were intensely flavored."

The flavors were also intensely chunky. Ben & Jerry's first tried to follow Herrell's example and mix in candy and cookies on demand at their scoop shop. But that approach did not work out. "They never mastered the technique and quickly decided it would be easier if Jerry put the chunks in while the ice cream was being cranked," Lager wrote. And the chunks were big. "I was advocating that a larger number of smaller chunks be well distributed throughout the ice cream," Greenfield told the *New York Times* in 2020. "Ben was insisting on bigger chunks. Ben was right." Ben & Jerry's added another ingredient to their premium ice cream: cheeky pun-filled names like Cherry Garcia and Chubby Hubby.

Around 1980, the pair began selling to wholesale customers—restaurants at first and then grocery stores. But it took a fight with competitor Häagen-Dazs in 1984 to put Ben & Jerry's on the map. A subsidiary of the Pillsbury Corporation, Häagen-Dazs dominated the super-premium ice cream market at the time. When the company threatened to drop distributors that also sold Ben & Jerry's, Cohen and Greenfield fought back. In addition to taking legal action, the pair launched a public relations

Did you know? Ben & Jerry's has a Flavor Graveyard for some of their "dearly de-pinted" flavors. Retired flavors include Dastardly Mash (chocolate ice cream with pecans, almonds, raisins and chocolate chips), Rainforest Crunch (ice cream with a cashew and Brazil nut brittle), Urban Jumble (a mix of chocolate and coconut ice cream with white and dark chocolate chunks, pecans and roasted almonds) and Holy Cannoli (ricotta and pistachio ice cream with chocolate-covered cannoli and roasted pistachios). The graveyard is located near the Ben & Jerry's factory in Waterbury, Vermont, and each departed flavor has a headstone and tongue-in-cheek epitaph.

campaign that asked, "What's the Doughboy Afraid Of?" The tagline, which referenced Pillsbury's famous mascot, was printed on Ben & Jerry's pint containers, plastered on buses and even towed by an airplane over the crowd at a Boston College football game. Customers could call a Doughboy Hotline and receive a Doughboy kit with a bumper sticker and templates for writing protest letters. The campaign garnered customer interest and national publicity; at one point, Ben & Jerry's was sending out four hundred Doughboy kits a week. The companies settled out of court in 1985 (with a brief complication in 1987). Pillsbury agreed not to coerce its distributors, and Ben & Jerry's agreed to end the Doughboy campaign.

From the early days of their company, Cohen and Greenfield incorporated social justice goals into their business model. The company's mission statement has three broad goals: (1) Make the finest quality ice cream, incorporating wholesome ingredients and respecting the environment; (2) Manage the company for sustainable financial growth; and (3) Use the company to make the world a better place.

Ben & Jerry's went public in 1984 and was acquired by corporate food giant Unilever in 2000 for about $326 million. Unilever agreed not to cut back the workforce or change the ice cream; a separate board was created to oversee the subsidiary. Cohen and Greenfield remained company employees although not in a management role. A year after the Unilever acquisition, Ben & Jerry's built a factory in Waterbury, Vermont. In 2012, Ben & Jerry's received B Corporation certification, which calls upon companies to meet social, economic and environmental standards. They were the first wholly owned subsidiary in the world to achieve this status.

As the *New York Times* wrote at the time of the Unilever deal, "Did Ben & Jerry's sell out, or is the Ben & Jerry's culture invading the corporate world? A scoop of each, perhaps." Twenty-plus years later, tensions between the parties have resulted in litigation, especially in relation to some of the positions Ben & Jerry's has taken regarding Middle East politics. In 2024, Unilever announced plans to spin off its ice cream holdings, which included Talenti, Wall's, Magnum and Ben & Jerry's.

TOSCANINI'S

Gus Rancatore grew up in New York and New Jersey and moved to Boston in 1973. That is when he discovered Steve's Ice Cream. One night at Steve's, after polishing off a dish of vanilla ice cream with mixed-in chocolate chips and hot fudge on top, Rancatore saw a help-wanted sign and applied for the job. He was hired as an overnight cleaner. After six months of cleaning up the detritus of ice cream making—hot fudge, strawberries and candy everywhere—he was promoted to scooper and then ice cream maker. "Right away, I loved making ice cream," Rancatore wrote in his memoir *Ice Cream Man*. "It's fun. It's a sensual experience and a childhood fantasy. You are Willy Wonka in your own little factory."

In 1981, Rancatore left Steve's (by then owned by the Crugnale brothers) and teamed up with Kurt Jaenicke, his siblings and other partners to open Toscanini's. The name was a nod to Jaenicke's grandfather, who had played in the conductor's orchestra. They located the shop in Central Square, a multicultural Cambridge neighborhood between Harvard University and the Massachusetts Institute of Technology. The Toscanini's storefront at 899 Main Street also put them at the edge of Confectioner's Row, and Rancatore recalled seeing Necco workers in their white uniforms and hairnets taking smoking breaks outside the factory.

For a while, Gus's brother Joe worked at Toscanini's, but they discovered they were not cut out to work together. "Now we cooperate on a lot of things," Gus said. "And we still agree to disagree and even agree to disagree about how we disagree." Joe left Toscanini's in 1985 and opened his own chain of ice cream shops called Rancatore's in three Boston suburbs: Belmont, Lexington and Newtonville. Their sister Mimi works with Gus at Toscanini's.

Thanks to high-quality ice cream and creative flavors, Toscanini's has been an enduring success. Rancatore credits listening to his customers and adapting to a changing market. "The mix of customers has become a lot more international, and younger people are more willing to eat across traditional boundaries," Rancatore told *Boston Magazine* in 2024. Besides familiar flavors like Belgian Chocolate, Strawberry, French Vanilla and Cookie Dough, Toscanini's offers B3 (its signature flavor combining brown butter, brown sugar and brownies), Kulfi (cardamom, almonds and pistachios), Green Tea (made with matcha), Halvah (sesame candy in sweet cream) and the delightfully named Milo Godzilla (based on a Singaporean drink made with sweetened condensed milk). Grape-Nut ice cream was a surprise hit. While he occasionally sells a scoop to someone from northern New England with a hankering for Grape-Nut pudding, Rancatore discovered the flavor was most popular with customers who hail from the West Indies.

Toscanini's ice cream shop in Cambridge, Massachusetts. *Courtesy of author.*

But running an ice cream shop is also about the people. In *Ice Cream Man*, Rancatore likened his role to "being the host of a B&B, or the director of a day-care center or, sometimes, a cop in a *Star Wars* bar." He continued, "Everyone is looking for connection, particularly in the sometimes harsh atmosphere of a large metropolitan area. If their car was towed, if the dog died, if the thesis was rejected, they should think that at least the person at the ice cream store was friendly and the Ginger Snap Molasses didn't disappoint them."

After forty-plus years at the helm of Toscanini's, Rancatore still loves what he does. "I enjoy the customer contact, and I enjoy making ice cream and coming up with flavors," he said. "One is very sociable, and the other one is relatively solitary."

J.P. Licks

A self-described "oddball from birth," Vince Petryk said his forty-year career in ice cream started by accident. After graduating from Temple University in 1976 with a degree in psychology, he started working at an ice cream shop in Philadelphia. He began as a dishwasher and worked his way up to manager and head ice cream maker. He spent a few years honing his management skills and opened J.P. Licks in an old firehouse in the Jamaica Plain neighborhood of Boston (hence the J.P.) in 1981. Today, J.P. Licks has seventeen locations.

J.P. Licks is known for its creative flavors (they have been described as "vivid" and "intense"); they include multiple variations on cookies-and-cream (mint, coffee, peanut butter and salted caramel cookies), brownie brownie batter and gingersnap molasses. But Petryk tries to offer something more than novel flavors, he told the *Boston Globe* in a 2016 profile; he also trades on nostalgia. "I realized when I was younger that ice cream connects you to some of the fondest memories of your childhood: The love you received from your parents and the happiest times spent with family and friends," he said.

EMACK & BOLIO'S

Emack & Bolio's has roots in Boston's rock-and-roll scene. In 1975, Robert Rook was a civil rights lawyer with a background in the music business. At the time, Boston's music clubs were required to shut down at midnight on Saturday nights thanks to a set of blue laws then on the books. Rook decided to create a space where musicians could hang out after their gigs, play some tunes and have a little fun. He rented a basement apartment in Brookline and invited his musician friends; to satisfy their post-midnight munchies, he started making ice cream.

In an interview with WERS-FM, he described what happened next: "After a few months of paying the rent and the electric and the ice cream bills, I thought maybe I should sell the ice cream instead of giving it away to my friends." So that is what he did. And while he had the ice cream and the location, the shop still needed a name. At the time, he was doing pro bono legal work for two homeless clients called Donald Emack and John Bolio. When he told them he was opening an ice cream shop, they asked him to name it after them.

Today, Emack & Bolio's has locations in the United States, Korea and China.

A FEW WORDS ABOUT MIX-INS

Whether they are called mix-ins or smoosh-ins, some ice cream add-in ingredients have achieved iconic status. Among them are Heath bars, chocolate chip cookie dough and Oreos.

Heath bars were among the most popular mix-ins at Steve's, and their story is a fascinating footnote in the scoop shop's history. The toffee-and-almond candy bars covered in milk chocolate were first sold in 1928 by L.S. Heath & Sons, a family-owned company in Illinois. According to a 1987 article in the *New York Times*, the candy was modestly successful—ranking fifty-sixth in candy and chewing gum sales—but its popularity skyrocketed with the advent of mix-ins, first at Steve's and then at Ben & Jerry's.

By the late 1980s, Ben & Jerry's was Heath's single largest customer, receiving a twenty-ton shipment every two weeks for its best-selling Heath Bar Crunch flavor. Jerry Greenfield described the magic combination of Heath bars and ice cream. "Some parts maintain their integrity as little chunks of Heath bar," he said. "Some parts turn to little pools of toffee within the ice cream, and others turn to liquid to form a light background flavor." The Hershey Company acquired Heath bars in 1996, and Ben & Jerry's switched to a different toffee bar supplier.

Cohen and Greenfield also take credit for introducing the world to chocolate chip cookie dough ice cream. As they tell the story, an anonymous customer suggested adding chunks of cookie dough to vanilla ice cream in 1984. The flavor was an immediate success at the Burlington scoop shop, but it took seven years to bring cookie dough to the packaged pints. Today, Chocolate Chip Cookie Dough is one of Ben & Jerry's most popular flavors.

Several people claim to have invented Cookies and Cream ice cream (often spelled Cookies 'n Cream)—including students at South Dakota State University—but nobody knows for certain where this enduring flavor originated. The flavor combines vanilla ice cream with chopped-up sandwich cookies. Many ice cream shops, including Steve's, at first, used Oreos until corporate owner Nabisco stepped in to protect its trademark. Toscanini's and Herrell's prefer to use Hydrox cookies, both for the taste and because Hydrox are kosher. (Oreos were made with lard into the 1990s but are kosher now.) Fun fact: the name for Hydrox cookies combined *hydrogen* and *oxygen*, the molecules that make up water, and was intended to suggest purity. Hydrox originated in 1908, and Oreos came along four years later.

Chapter 9

OFFICIAL SWEETS AND RUNNERS-UP

Whoopie Pies, Lollipops and Marshmallow Fluff

The official sweets for the New England states (including a few also-rans) make up an eclectic mix of traditional baked goods and syrupy delights. Maine has honored three foods with official status: wild blueberry pie is the official dessert, whoopie pies are the official treat and maple syrup is the official sweetener. Massachusetts named Boston Cream Pie as the official state dessert (and its variation Boston Cream Doughnut as the official doughnut) and the Toll House cookie as the official state cookie. Rhode Island designated coffee milk as its official state beverage, and Connecticut claimed the lollipop as its state candy in 2024. Vermont chose apple pie as its state pie and maple syrup as its official flavor. New Hampshire does not have a state dessert, but pumpkin is the official state fruit. Many think the snickerdoodle is the official Connecticut cookie, but it has no official status. Neither does the Fig Newton or the Fluffernutter sandwich, despite an enthusiastic following in Massachusetts.

WHOOPIE PIES

Like another classic New England sweet, a whoopie pie is not a pie. (Looking at you, Boston Cream Pie.) Instead, picture two mounds of chocolate cake surrounding a white creamy filling.

Three states can credibly claim the whoopie pie as their own: Maine, Pennsylvania and Massachusetts. Each traces the treat to the 1920s.

Maine's connection to whoopie pies is centered in Lewiston, and Labadie's Bakery is considered ground zero. The family-owned bakery sold its first whoopie pie in 1925 and still follows the same recipe. Today, Labadie's offers whoopie pies in several flavors, including the original chocolate, and supplies multiple retail outlets, mail-order sales and walk-in customers. The Labadie's origin story is widely accepted throughout Maine, although it should be noted that the bakery's paper records were destroyed in a fire.

Not so fast, say Pennsylvanians. Some folks in the Keystone State trace the whoopie pie to the Harris-Boyer bakery in Johnstown. According to the story, a bakery worker made himself a sandwich of sorts, with two small chocolate cakes and a layer of icing in between. Bakery managers liked what they saw and began selling the treat. Harris-Boyer called them gob cakes, perhaps after the slang coal mining term for a lump of refuse material, and trademarked the term *gob* in 1927. Another tale puts whoopie pies in the kitchens of home bakers in the Pennsylvania Amish community. The cakes were a practical way to make use of leftover batter, and women were said to tuck the treats into the lunchboxes of their husbands and children, who exclaimed "Whoopie!" when they found the desserts.

Labadie's Bakery in Lewiston, Maine, has been making whoopie pies since 1925. *Courtesy of author.*

Whatever the origins, Pennsylvanians have adopted whoopie pies as their own.

The Massachusetts whoopie pie story requires a detour through North Berwick, Maine, and the once storied Berwick cake. In the nineteenth century, North Berwick was a busy station on the Boston and Maine Railroad. When the trains stopped to take on water, passengers often sampled a lemony sponge cake at a nearby restaurant owned by Mary Ann Pettengill and her husband, William Briggs. An 1896 story in the *Portland Transcript* shared the origins of the popular cake. One day in the 1860s, a woman identified as Mrs. B (presumably Mary Ann Pettengill Briggs) was interrupted while making a cake. While she was out of the kitchen, her young daughter added something—never identified but possibly cream of tartar—to the batter. Mrs. B baked the cake anyway, and the soon-to-be famous Berwick sponge cake was born. Pettengill made a tidy living from selling the cake and passed the secret recipe to her son-in-law shortly before she died in 1898. The son-in-law sold the recipe to the Oak Grove Farm Creamery in Roxbury, Massachusetts.

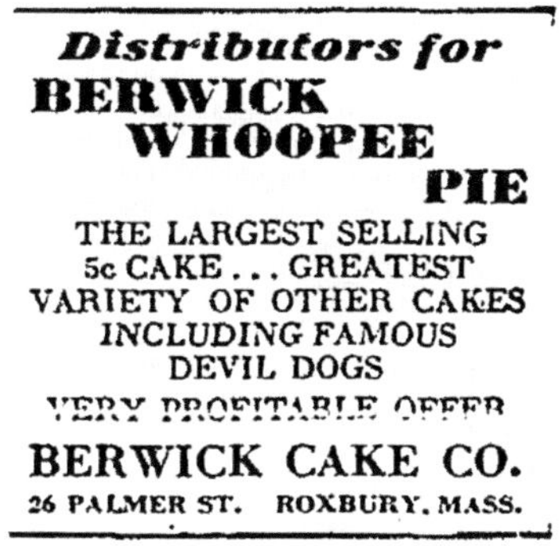

Early advertisement for the Berwick Cake Company highlighting whoopie pies and Devil Dogs. *Author's collection.*

After acquiring the recipe, the creamery changed its name to the Berwick Cake Company and began making its new namesake confection. Sometime between 1926 and 1931, Berwick added whoopie pies to its offerings. It is not known whether Berwick got the recipe from bakers in Maine or Pennsylvania or developed the product in-house. Some suggest that another Berwick confection inspired whoopie pies. Berwick had already created a chocolate cake with a marshmallow filling in the 1920s. The cakes were shaped like hot dog buns and were dubbed "Devil Dogs." Details are scarce and contradictory, but Berwick supposedly sold the recipe to Drake Bakeries, which still makes Devil Dogs. Drake's began using the name Devil Dogs in June 1926 and applied for trademark protection in October of that year. Although the Drake's website makes no mention of the product's Boston origins, a 1931 ad for Berwick Cake Company refers to "famous Devil Dogs."

The Berwick origin story has a delicious musical theater twist. In October 1928, a stage show called *Whoopee* starring Eddie Cantor and produced by Florenz Ziegfeld came to Boston. As the story goes, the crew handed out whoopie pies to audience members as Cantor sang "Makin' Whoopee." Whether the cake or the song came first hardly matters; it was a match made in confectionery heaven.

Another Massachusetts origin story ties the treat to the company that makes Marshmallow Fluff. Some say a whoopie pie recipe appeared in the *Yummy Book*, a recipe collection Durkee-Mower started publishing in 1930. Some cooks use Fluff as a filling in their whoopie pies, which gives the tale some credibility. But Don Durkee, son of one of the firm's founders, debunked the *Yummy* connection. "I'm baffled," he told the *New York Times* in 2009. He said whoopie pies did not appear in the company's recipe pamphlets until the 1970s.

Did you know? Former Maine state senator Justin Chenette was inspired by the legislative process to name whoopie pies the official state treat and wrote *The Great Whoopie Pie Debate: A Kid's Guide to the Maine Legislature.* The book, with illustrations by Jefferson Coniaris, takes students from a fictional classroom to the state capitol in Augusta to learn how their state government works.

No matter where they originated, whoopie pies are embedded in the culinary cultures of both Maine and Pennsylvania. Not surprisingly, both states have whoopie pie festivals. Pennsylvania was first, and the Hershey Farms Resort in Ronks has hosted a whoopie pie festival since 2005. Maine has held its whoopie pie festival since 2008 as a benefit for the Center Theatre in Dover-Foxcroft. Joining the whoopie bandwagon, Rutland, Vermont, started its own whoopie pie festival in 2022.

While traditionalists stick with the chocolate whoopie with a vanilla filling (usually buttercream or Fluff), whoopie pies lend themselves to endless variations. A sampling of whoopies from the 2024 Dover-Foxcroft festival includes pumpkin, blueberry-lemon, orange creamsicle, strawberry shortcake, birthday cake, Earl Grey tea and bubble gum.

The sweet, sticky pies are widely available, but a few Maine bakeries have staked out a reputation in the world of whoopies. WICKED WHOOPIES started more than twenty-five years ago. The company has a storefront in Freeport and makes about ten thousand whoopie pies a day in its bakery in Gardiner. CAPE WHOOPIES, with a retail bakery in South Portland, bills itself as "Maine's gourmet pie." TWO FAT CATS BAKERY has locations in Portland and South Portland; the spot specializes in sweet treats baked from scratch, including whoopie pies and wild blueberry pie. In Kennebunk, Auntie's House sells traditional whoopie pies along with a confection they call the Whoopie Ball. A Whoopie Ball is a whoopie pie about the size and shape of a golf ball; the treat has a creamy filling and is dipped in chocolate.

Whoopie pies were named the official Maine state treat in 2011, but the designation was anything but assured. At first, legislators tried to name whoopie pies the official state dessert. But opposition from fans of the wild blueberry derailed that proposal, and a compromise was reached. The whoopie pie would be the official state treat, and wild blueberry pie would be the official state dessert. Governor Paul LePage did not sign the whoopie pie bill, claiming he had more important concerns, but the designation took effect in 2011 without his imprimatur.

WILD BLUEBERRY PIE

The wild blueberry has thrived in the harsh climate, acidic soil and rocky terrain of Maine and eastern Canada for thousands of years. Wabanaki tribes relied on the berries for food and medicine and believed the fruit had magical powers. European colonists came to enjoy the berries and incorporated them in everything from baked goods to paint.

A Mrs. Bliss, who did not share her first name, is believed to have published the first recipe for blueberry pie in her 1850 book, *The Practical Cook Book*. But wild blueberries remained something of a local secret until the American Civil War. Southern U.S. states were once a major market for Maine's sardine canneries. The market dried up after war broke out, and some canneries pivoted to produce tinned blueberries for Union troops. Soldiers developed a taste for the sweet berries, and demand for the fruit grew beyond Maine.

Because wild blueberries, known as lowbush varieties, cannot be cultivated and do not travel well, the search was on to develop a more commercially viable variety. The first hybrid blueberries were developed in New Jersey in the early 1900s (where they were named the official state fruit in 2004). The new berries, dubbed "highbush," quickly became successful and are now cultivated around the world. Color aside, the two berries should not be confused. Wild blueberries are smaller and sweeter than their hybrid counterparts, and their flavor is more intense.

The Maine state legislature designated blueberry pie—made with wild blueberries, of course—the official state dessert in 2011.

APPLE PIE

It may seem counterintuitive, but apple pie—the quintessential American dessert—originated in England. Apples were not native to North America, but European colonists brought apple seeds with them, and the transplanted crop flourished.

At first, the colonists used apples mostly for making cider. But other uses caught on, and early American cookbook author Amelia Simmons included two recipes for apple pie in her 1796 recipe book *American Cookery*—one with a top crust and one without. Here is her recipe for the former: "Pare, quarter and core tart apples, lay in paste No. 3, cover with the same; bake half an hour, when drawn, gently raise the top crust, add sugar, butter, cinnamon, mace, wine or rose-water." (Paste No. 3 is a pie crust.)

Fast-forward to 1999, when Vermont legislators named apple pie as the official state pie. An unofficial addendum to the legislation, probably a tongue-in-cheek attempt to boost the state's dairy industry, included the following instructions: "When serving apple pie in Vermont, a 'good faith' effort shall be made to meet one or more of the following conditions: (a) with a glass of cold milk, (b) with a slice of cheddar cheese weighing a minimum of ½ ounce, or (c) with a large scoop of vanilla ice cream."

PUMPKIN PIE

Pumpkins are native to Central America, and European explorers brought them back from the New World in the 1500s. English cooks soon began using *pomions*, as they called them, in sweet and savory pastries. In fact, it is likely that the Pilgrims who landed on Plymouth Rock in 1620 were just as familiar with pumpkin as the Wampanoag Natives who greeted them. Scholars believe pumpkin was on the menu for the so-called first Thanksgiving, a harvest feast in 1621 with Pilgrim settlers and Wampanoags in attendance, but pumpkin pie as we know it was not.

By the eighteenth century, Thanksgiving had become an important New England holiday, and pumpkin pie was part of the tradition. In 1796, Amelia Simmons included two recipes for pumpkin pudding (or "pompkin" as the spelling evolved) in *American Cookery*. One resembled the modern pumpkin custard pie and read: "One quart of milk, 1 pint pompkin, 4 eggs, molasses, allspice and ginger in a crust, bake 1 hour."

Pumpkin pie has yet to achieve official state status in New England, but New Hampshire designated pumpkin as the official state fruit in 2006.

BOSTON CREAM PIE

The first thing to know about Boston Cream Pie is that it is not a pie at all. The dessert is two layers of sponge cake with a vanilla cream filling and covered with chocolate fondant.

The second thing to know is that the cake changed the way Americans thought about chocolate. Although chocolate was readily available in the nineteenth century, most people still consumed their chocolate as a beverage.

The third thing to know is that a chef at the Parker House may have invented the dessert, and the hotel certainly popularized it. After Harvey Parker opened his hotel in downtown Boston in 1855, he hired a French chef named Augustine François Anezin (sometimes spelled Sanzian) at what was then an extravagant salary of $5,000 a year to create a menu befitting the grand setting. In 1856 (or possibly the 1860s), Anezin introduced a dessert called Chocolate Cream Pie, which featured chocolate icing on top of a round sponge cake with a vanilla custard filling. The dessert was a variation on several cakes popular at the time, including Washington Pie, which was a round cake filled with jam and dusted with sugar. But using chocolate in a cake was revolutionary.

But why is this cake called a pie? The most common explanation is that early American cooks mostly made pies. When cakes became popular, home cooks simply baked them in their readily available pie pans.

Boston Cream Pie, still sold at the Omni Parker House, was named the official Massachusetts dessert in 1996, and even Julia Child approved. When the *Boston Globe* asked her to comment on the designation, she said, "Well why not? It's called Boston cream pie. It's quite fitting. A cheesecake wouldn't make sense." The Boston Cream Doughnut followed as the official state doughnut in 2003.

TOLL HOUSE COOKIES

Ruth and Kenneth Wakefield ran the Toll House Restaurant in Whitman, Massachusetts, from 1930 through 1967. The restaurant had a devoted following and was a popular stopping place for vacationers heading toward Cape Cod. Joe DiMaggio, Cole Porter, Joseph Kennedy Sr. and Eleanor Roosevelt were said to be fans.

An accomplished cook, Ruth Wakefield is best known for inventing the Toll House Cookie in the late 1930s. Originally called the Toll House Chocolate Crunch Cookie, the recipe first appeared in the 1938 edition of her book, *Tried and True Recipes*. The thin and crunchy cookies were intended to be served alongside ice cream.

Toll House Chocolate Crunch Cookie

Cream 1 cup butter, add ¾ cup brown sugar, ¾ cup granulated sugar, and 2 eggs beaten whole.
Dissolve 1 tsp. soda in 1 tsp. hot water and mix alternately with 2¼ cups flour sifted with 1 tsp. salt.
Lastly add 1 cup chopped nuts and 2 bars (7-oz.) Nestlés yellow label chocolate, semi-sweet, which has been cut in pieces the size of a pea.
Flavor with 1 tsp. vanilla and drop half teaspoons on a greased cookie sheet.
Bake 10 to 12 minutes in a 375-degree oven.
Makes 100 cookies.

Newspapers reprinted the recipe, and Wakefield was featured on radio shows. The cookies tapped into the national mood and became wildly popular. Jon Michaud described some of the appeal in the *New Yorker*:

> *Wakefield's cookie was the perfect antidote to the Great Depression. In a single inexpensive hand-held serving, it contained the very richness and comfort that millions of people were forced to live without in the late nineteen-thirties. Ingesting a warm chocolate-chip cookie offered the eaters a brief respite from their quotidian woe.*

As the popularity of the recipe grew, so did demand for Nestlé's semisweet chocolate bars. Nestlé offered to print Wakefield's recipe on the chocolate bar wrapper, rebranded as Nestlé Toll House Chocolate Chip Cookies. Wakefield supposedly received one dollar, free chocolate for life and publicity for the fourth edition of her cookbook. Soon Nestlé added scoring marks to make the chocolate easier to chop and, starting in 1941, manufactured the familiar drop-shaped chocolate chips. Carolyn Wyman, who wrote *The Great American Chocolate Chip Cookie Book*, called Nestlé chocolate chips "the only really highly successful food product that was made just for a specific recipe."

Stories began to circulate saying that Wakefield developed the cookies by accident. Some claim that she added chocolate bits to the recipe when she ran out of nuts. Others say the vibrations of an industrial mixer caused some chocolate pieces to fall into the batter. These stories are most likely urban legends. Speaking on the *Gastropod* podcast, author and pastry chef Stella Parks called the theories "patronizing and insulting." She continued, "Ruth Wakefield was a bestselling cookbook author, an entrepreneur, a very successful businesswoman, incredibly savvy with decades of experience in the kitchen." The *New York Times* backs this up. In the "Overlooked" series of obituaries, the *Times* wrote:

> *Legend had it that she was brainstorming about cookie dough while returning from a vacation in Egypt when she first came up with the recipe, a variation on another popular treat called Butter Drop Do pecan icebox cookies. "We had been serving a thin butterscotch nut cookie with ice cream," Wakefield recalled in a 1970s interview. "Everybody seemed to love it, but I was trying to give them something different."*

But then the *Times* revived one of the urban myths about the accidental invention. Wakefield planned to add melted Baker's chocolate to the butterscotch batter, according to the story, but the baking chocolate was not on hand. Instead, she used an ice pick to chop up a bar of Nestlé's semisweet chocolate and, having no time to melt it, added it to the cookie dough. The chocolate bits did not melt completely, and the chocolate chip cookie was born.

Complicating these accounts, there is evidence that chocolate chip cookies were around before Wakefield created her recipe. Parks said supermarket chains like Kroger were selling chocolate chip cookies by the pound in the 1930s.

But no matter who invented the treat, there is no doubt that Ruth Wakefield's Toll House recipe and her partnership with Nestlé made chocolate chip cookies an American classic.

The Wakefields sold the Toll House in 1967, and the restaurant burned down in 1984. Massachusetts recognized Ruth Wakefield's creation as the official state cookie in 1997, beating out the Fig Newton for the honor.

FIG NEWTONS

Fig rolls were once considered a health food. In the nineteenth century, these soft biscuits filled with fig jam were thought to aid digestion. They were popular with home cooks across Great Britain, and British immigrants likely brought the biscuits to the United States. But it took a fortuitous combination of a cookie maker turned real estate developer from Ohio, an inventor in Philadelphia and a bakery in Massachusetts to turn the humble fig roll into the Fig Newton, one of the best-selling cookies in the country.

Artemus Kennedy (sometimes spelled Artemas) founded a bakery on Main Street in Cambridge around 1840 that produced crackers. When Kennedy died in 1861, his twenty-year-old son Frank Artemus Kennedy took over. The younger Kennedy expanded the business and moved to a new factory on Franklin Street in 1875; he called it the F.A. Kennedy Steam Bakery.

Kennedy Biscuit Works, as the company was sometimes called, produced a range of cookies and crackers but is best known for introducing the Fig Newton. And that is where the Ohio cookie maker and the Philadelphia inventor come in.

Charles Martin Roser was an Ohioan who was widely credited with developing the recipe for a fig cookie that he sold to Kennedy, although the details are sketchy. Roser eventually settled in St. Petersburg, Florida, where he became a real estate developer and philanthropist.

James Henry Mitchell was a Philadelphia inventor who developed a machine that could fill a cookie crust with fruit. Some sources say he sold his machine to Kennedy Biscuit Works; others say he worked there. Either way, this machine was the key to taking fig rolls from the home kitchen to the assembly line.

Did you know? The City of Newton has embraced its role in cookie history. Newton's long-serving Mayor Theodore D. Mann was known to keep a stash of the cookies in his office and hand them out to visitors. In 1991, Nabisco staged a centennial celebration in the city featuring a barbecue, giant Fig Newton cookie and entertainment. Mann was the enthusiastic host. "You don't hear about Fig Philadelphias or Fig New Yorks," he said at the time. Subsequent mayors continued the tradition of sharing Fig Newtons with guests.

The baker, the recipe and the technology were the magical combination that brought the new cookie to market. Introduced in 1891, Fig Newtons were named after the nearby city of Newton, one of many Kennedy products named after Massachusetts communities, including the Shrewsbury, the Melrose, the Brighton and Cambridge Salts.

In 1898, the New York Biscuit Company and the American Biscuit and Manufacturing Company merged over one hundred bakeries—including Kennedy Biscuit Works—into the National Biscuit Company, now called

Nabisco. Nabisco occupied the Cambridge factory for decades. The company still makes Fig Newtons but dropped "Fig" from the cookie name in 2012. Kennedy Biscuit Works was converted to housing and placed on the National Register of Historic Places.

Fig Newtons almost became the official Massachusetts state cookie in 1997 thanks to the lobbying efforts of then Governor William F. Weld. Although state legislators supported the Toll House cookie, Weld was a fan of the soft fruit cookie. "Everybody I knew grew up with Fig Newtons," he said. "The packaging is distinct, they're delicious. I think out of respect for Teddy Mann, that alone should lead us to cast our lot with the Fig Newton." But Weld was in the minority on this issue and ultimately signed the Toll House designation into law.

LOLLIPOPS

Lollipops were invented in New Haven, Connecticut—or maybe not. Like the stories behind many classic sweets, the details are a little fuzzy.

George Smith, of the Bradley Smith Company on Grand Street in New Haven, began producing lollipops in 1908. He reportedly was inspired by a chocolate caramel candy on a stick called Reynolds Taffy and produced in nearby West Haven. He called his sweets Lolly Pops after a racehorse, and he used hard candy instead of caramel.

The first Lolly Pops were formed by hand. Employees took a blob of warm candy, jammed a stick into it and flattened the warm ball with their palms. The game changed when Max Buchmueller, a Bradley Smith employee, invented a machine to automate the process of inserting sticks into the candy. The Buchmueller Candy-Making Machine, patented in 1914, enabled the company to produce 125 Lolly Pops a minute; later improvements increased output to 750 pops per minute.

Smith tried to trademark the Lolly Pop name but ran into roadblocks. His first application was rejected because government researchers found the term was used in the 1800s to describe "a hard sweetmeat sometimes on a stick." But Smith was persistent, and the name Lolly Pop was finally registered to the Bradley Smith Company in 1931. Unfortunately for Smith, the word *lollipop* was widely used by then, and the trademark was unenforceable. The company went bankrupt during the Great Depression (or shortly after) and was reconfigured as a wholesale candy distributor.

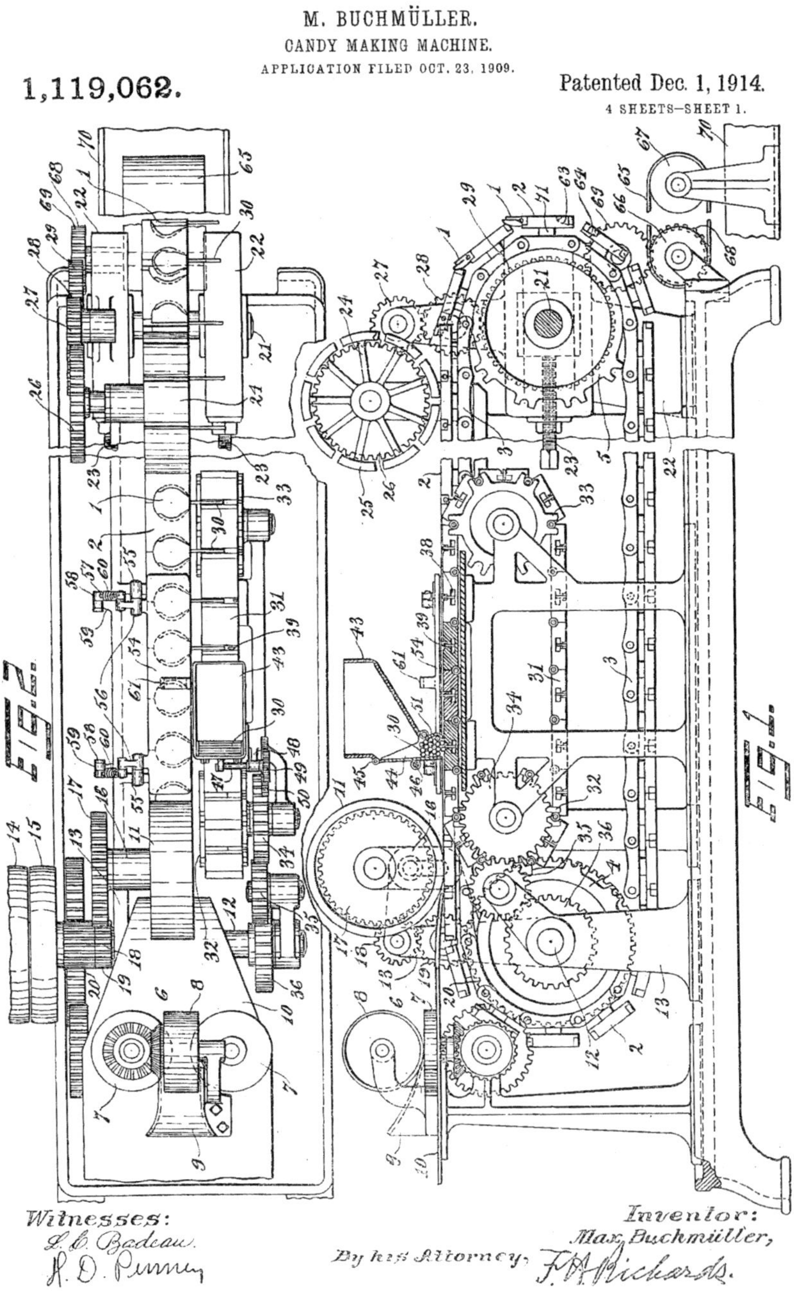

Detail from the patent application for Max Buchmueller's lollipop machine. *Courtesy of U.S. Patent and Trademark Office.*

But is that the whole story? A blog post from Candy Creek Lollipops suggests that the McAviney Candy Company, another Connecticut confectioner, created the modern lollipop:

> *As the story goes, this happened almost by accident. The employees would use wooden sticks to stir the candy as it cooked, and throughout the day candy would accumulate on the stick. By the end of each day, there would be many left over "candy sticks" which employees would bring home to their children. Soon they started selling these candy sticks to the public.*

More than one hundred years later, it is impossible to know which story is true (if either). Further raising questions about Bradley Smith's accomplishments, two other companies invented machines to place candy on a stick around the same time. In 1908, the Wisconsin-based Racine Confectionery Machine Company created the Racine Automatic Sucker Machine, and in 1912, Samuel Born (who later came up with chocolate sprinkles) invented the Born Sucker Machine while he was in California.

But Connecticut has embraced the lollipop as its own, even if the provenance is a little sketchy. The lollipop was designated as the state candy in 2024.

COFFEE SYRUP

Chocolate milk may be a familiar beverage in forty-nine states of the Union, but many Rhode Islanders grew up with coffee milk instead.

Coffee milk is exactly what it sounds like: milk flavored with coffee syrup. Coffee syrup is sweetened, concentrated coffee that resembles chocolate syrup. Many speculate that the beverage originated in Rhode Island's Italian and Portuguese immigrant communities, but no one knows for certain.

By the 1930s, companies in Rhode Island and southeastern Massachusetts were manufacturing coffee syrup, and coffee milk was available at soda fountains and diners. "The lure of the grown-up beverage, combined with the one-two punch of sugar and caffeine, made the stuff a sure-fire hit," the Quahog.org website posted. "Kids liked it because of its adult mystique and because it tasted good. Parents liked it because it was a way to get their kids to drink milk."

The Silmo Packing Company, named after its founders, Louis Silva and Carlos Desouza Morais, began manufacturing coffee syrup in New Bedford, Massachusetts, in 1932. Eclipse Food Products introduced coffee syrup in 1938 in Warwick, Rhode Island, with the slogan "You smack your lips if it's Eclipse." In Lincoln, Rhode Island, Autocrat coffee syrup ("A swallow will tell you") hit the market in 1940. Eclipse and Autocrat duked it out in the Ocean State until 1991, when Autocrat acquired Eclipse and another brand called Coffee Time. Autocrat was acquired by the British tea company James Finlay Limited in 2014 and still retails all three coffee syrups under their individual brand names. Silmo hung on through several ownership changes, even renaming its product MilkMate in 1996, but could not compete with Autocrat; the Massachusetts company closed up shop in 2000.

Today, a coffee syrup renaissance is underway. In New Bedford, city councilor Ian Abreu is reviving Silmo syrup. His grandfather Manny Martin owned the company from 1970 through 1989, and the family acquired the original Silmo recipe and the rights to distribute the product. "People have had a hankering for it for quite some time," Abreu told the *Standard-Times*. "People would say to me to bring it back over the last couple of years. As is anything in life, it just wasn't the right time." The time was finally right in 2022, and Silmo hit the shelves again for the first time in two decades. Also in Massachusetts, David and Mary Silvia began making Morning Glory Old Fashioned Coffee Syrup in 2001 from their home in Dartmouth. Using a family recipe, they originally gave away bottles of syrup as Christmas gifts, but the positive response convinced them to go into business. And in Rhode Island, Dave Lanning opened a coffee bar called Dave's Coffee in Charlestown in 2006. The company began roasting its own beans in

Did you know? In 1975, George Howell opened a small café in Harvard Square called the Coffee Connection. In 1992, he experimented with iced cappuccino drinks and came up with a creamy version that used ice, espresso, milk and coffee milk. Howell coined a name that combined *cappuccino* and *frappe*—and the Frappuccino was born. The new drink fueled the expansion of Coffee Connection, and Starbucks took notice. The Seattle company acquired the Northeastern chain—and the rights to the Frappuccino—in 1994, and Autocrat came along for the ride. The Rhode Island company supplied the coffee syrup that powered Frappuccinos for years, until Starbucks took syrup production in-house.

2012, and Lanning experimented with making coffee syrup. "I really wanted to focus on the quality of the beans and to only use coffee and cane sugar," he said. "It took some tinkering, but we ended up with a formula using nutty, chocolatey Brazilian beans that pair so perfectly with the sugar." Even Dunkin' Donuts jumped on the coffee milk bandwagon in 2024. The chain tapped into its New England roots to introduce the Dunkalatte in 2004—a latte made with coffee milk. The coffee syrup was the brand's own blend.

Coffee milk was declared the official Rhode Island state beverage in 1993, beating back a strong challenge from Del's Frozen Lemonade. "This great state was founded on the principles of rugged individualism, and we're proud of the things that make us different from people in other places," state senator John W. Lyle declared in a legislative session. "Coffee milk is one of those things."

Maple Syrup

European settlers learned about maple syrup from the Native Abenaki people, who had long been turning maple sap into sweeteners. Although the colonists were not familiar with maple trees, they quickly mastered the sugaring process and over the centuries transformed maple sugaring into a major industry and tourist attraction.

Turning maple sap into sugar or syrup is labor intensive, slow and seasonal. Maple trees produce sap in the early spring, and a typical sugaring season lasts from four to six weeks. Workers drill a tap hole into a tree and insert a spout or tubing to collect the sap. A tree must be about forty years old before it can be tapped. The sap is collected and then boiled in a pan called an evaporator, sometimes after a process to remove some of its water, until it reaches 219 degrees Fahrenheit. Then the syrup is drawn off, filtered and graded for color and

Did you know? In 1791, Thomas Jefferson planted a maple orchard at his Monticello estate in Virginia. He was influenced by Dr. Benjamin Rush, a Philadelphia abolitionist, who supported the use of maple sugar instead of the cane product as a strategy to end sugar slavery in the West Indies. Unfortunately, most of the trees in Jefferson's maple grove did not survive, and his experiment in sugaring failed.

Checking the consistency of maple syrup, circa 1940. *Photo by Marion Post Wolcott, courtesy of Library of Congress.*

taste. It takes forty gallons of sap to make one gallon of maple syrup. In 2024, Vermont produced over two million gallons of maple syrup, top in the United States.

Maple syrup is a twofer. Vermont designated maple syrup as the official state flavor in 1993, and Maine selected maple syrup as the official state sweetener in 2015. Naturally, each state specified the syrup within its borders.

SNICKERDOODLES

Snickerdoodles are spice cookies with a silly name. Many people associate them with the state of Connecticut, and some even believe snickerdoodles are the Connecticut state cookie. But there is no direct evidence linking the cookies to the state, and they have not achieved official recognition.

Snickerdoodles can be traced to Dutch-German immigrants in Pennsylvania. The cookies captured the American imagination after New

York City cooking teacher and newspaper columnist Cornelia Campbell Bedford published a recipe in 1891 for sugar cookies sprinkled with cinnamon and sugar.

A staffer working in the Betty Crocker Homemaking Service Department at Washburn-Crosby Company (now General Mills) is also credited with popularizing the cookie. Minnesota native Patricia Anfinson got her dream job at Betty Crocker in 1945. Anfinson worked on *Betty Crocker's Picture Cook Book* and contributed her grandmother's recipe for snickerdoodles. "It's one of my happy childhood memories," the recipe introduction read. "My mother would be baking when we came home from school, and we would have Snickerdoodles hot out of the oven with a glass of milk." Anfinson left Betty Crocker a few years later, but she was forever known as the "Snickerdoodle Lady."

Snickerdoodle recipes call for flour, butter and/or shortening, eggs, sugar, salt, cinnamon and a leavening agent. The balls of dough are rolled in a mixture of sugar and cinnamon before baking, and the soft, chewy cookies come out of the oven with a crinkly top and crispy sides and bottom. The leavening agent—usually a combination of baking soda and cream of tartar—sets the cookies apart. Lifestyle guru Martha Stewart explained why:

> *Purists believe the cream of tartar is key to the snickerdoodle's chewy texture and its delightful, slightly tangy taste. Cream of tartar activates the baking soda and keeps sugar crystals from forming, so the cookies end up pillowy rather than crisp. Non-purists believe it's the cinnamon-sugar itself that accounts for the appeal of the cookie, and leave the cream of tartar out, replacing it with baking powder for leavening.*

As for the name, some trace the moniker to the German cinnamon rolls called *schneckennudeln* (literally "snail noodles") because of their spiral shape. Others say snickerdoodle is just a nonsense word. Food editor and author Judith Jones subscribed to the latter theory and wrote, "New England cooks had a penchant for giving odd names to their dishes—apparently for no other reason than the fun of saying them."

MARSHMALLOW FLUFF

Marshmallow Fluff is a sweet white gooey spread used as an ingredient in everything from fudge to whoopie pies—and sometimes eaten straight from the jar.

Archibald Query was a French-Canadian immigrant living in Somerville, Massachusetts, around the turn of the twentieth century. He sold homemade confections door to door, including a marshmallow cream he developed in 1917. But World War I sugar shortages forced Query to find other employment, and he began working at the Walter M. Lowney Company's factory on Commercial Street in Boston.

Fred L. Mower and H. Allen Durkee were childhood friends who grew up in Swampscott, Massachusetts. They both served in France during World War I. Back from the war, Mower also began working at Lowney's and befriended Query. It was a fortuitous connection. Mower and Durkee purchased Query's marshmallow cream recipe for $500 and opened the Durkee-Mower Company on Valentine's Day in 1920.

Durkee-Mower began manufacturing the product from a factory in Swampscott. They called it Toot Sweet Marshmallow Fluff in a punny reference to their time in France. The original recipe consisted of four ingredients: sugar, corn syrup, egg whites and vanilla. What made their Fluff so fluffy? That is still a trade secret.

By 1929, Marshmallow Fluff (the Toot Sweet branding had disappeared by then) was a hit, and Durkee-Mower needed more space. The company bought out Rich's Instant Cocoa (eventually renamed "Sweeco") and took over the hot cocoa's manufacturing facility in Lynn. Sweeco was discontinued in 1962, but Durkee-Mower is still in the Lynn factory (which has expanded over the years).

Query was not the first confectioner to make marshmallow cream, and Durkee-Mower was not the first commercial producer. Just a few miles from Somerville, siblings Emma and Amory Curtis (who happened to be descendants of Paul Revere) established the Emma E. Curtis Company around 1910 in Melrose; Snowflake Marshmallow Crème was their signature product. Meanwhile, Whitman's produced Marshmallow Whip in Philadelphia, and Hippolyte Marshmallow Creme was popular in the American South.

Most significantly, however, a confectionery company in New Jersey called Limpert Brothers also made a product called Marshmallow Fluff at roughly the same time as Durkee-Mower launched its product. In 1939, the

Durkee-Mower makes Marshmallow Fluff in this factory in Lynn, Massachusetts. *Courtesy of author.*

two companies agreed to share the product name under specific conditions. Durkee-Mower would continue to sell its Marshmallow Fluff to retail customers in New England with restrictions beyond the region; Limpert would continue to distribute its Marshmallow Fluff to commercial customers with no geographic restrictions.

Fred Mower passed away in 1957 at the age of fifty-nine. Durkee's sons Bruce and Don took on added leadership roles, and the team sharpened the company's focus. Sweeco was phased out, and Durkee-Mower turned its attention to expanding the Marshmallow Fluff market. One idea was to market a sandwich made with Fluff and peanut butter. Mimi Graney described the spark of genius in *Fluff: The Sticky Sweet Story of an American Icon*: "Durkee-Mower knew parents would be more inclined to support a steady marshmallow cream habit if it was part of a meal—like a sandwich made with nutritious peanut butter. And even the youngest child could execute a simple sandwich recipe."

But the real genius was the name: Fluffernutter. Durkee-Mower had been building brand awareness for Fluff with media sponsorships and advertisements for years. But Marshmallow Fluff did not achieve iconic status until Durkee-Mower rolled out the Fluffernutter in 1958.

Durkee-Mower did not invent the combination of peanut butter and marshmallow cream; Emma Curtis had earlier published a recipe for a similar sandwich she called the Liberty Sandwich. But the Fluffernutter name—and a catchy advertising jingle—proved irresistible, and Fluffernutters became a favorite of schoolchildren across New England.

Jump ahead to 2006, which was both a low point and a high point for Marshmallow Fluff. The low point came when Massachusetts state senator Jarrett Barrios learned that the Fluffernutter sandwich was available in the Cambridge Public Schools, where his sons were enrolled. Apparently, students could request a Fluffernutter as an alternative to the standard cafeteria fare. Barrios filed legislation to limit the Fluff option to one day per week and unleashed a firestorm. The Barrios story made international news and became fodder for late-night comedians; the senator was inundated with angry letters and telephone calls and even received death threats. State representative Kathi-Anne Reinstein, whose district included Lynn, filed a bill to designate the Fluffernutter the official state sandwich. The controversy eventually faded away, the proposed legislation did not pass, the Fluffernutter did not achieve official state status and Barrios resigned from the State Senate in 2007.

Also in 2006, Marshmallow Fluff celebrated its Somerville origins. That year, Union Square Main Streets hosted a street festival to honor Marshmallow Fluff and Archibald Query. Called "What the Fluff? A Tribute to Union Square Invention," the festival became an annual event and has drawn enthusiastic crowds ever since.

BIBLIOGRAPHY

Books

Almond, Steve. *Candyfreak: A Journey Through the Chocolate Underbelly of America.* Algonquin Books, 2004.

Benjamin, Susan. *Sweet as Sin: The Unwrapped Story of How Candy Became America's Favorite Pleasure.* Prometheus Books, 2016.

Bredeson, Carmen. *The Chocolate Chip Cookie Queen: Ruth Wakefield and Her Yummy Invention.* Enslow Elementary, 2014.

Broekel, Ray. *The Great American Candy Bar Book.* Houghton Mifflin Company, 1982.

Chenette, Justin. *The Great Whoopie Pie Debate.* Independently published, Bryson Taylor Publishing, n.d.

Commonwealth of Massachusetts Bureau of Statistics. *A Directory of Massachusetts Manufactures 1913.* Wright & Potter Printing Company, 1913.

Graney, Mimi. *Fluff: The Sticky Sweet Story of an American Icon.* Union Park Press, 2017.

Griffin, Nancy. *Making Whoopies: The Official Whoopie Pie Book.* Down East Books, 2010.

Herrell, Steve. *Ice Cream and Me.* Self-published, Not Too Shabby Publishing, 2021.

Kimmerle, Beth. *Candy: The Sweet History.* Collectors Press, 2007.

———. *Chocolate: The Sweet History.* Collectors Press, 2005.

Lacey, Darlene. *Necco: An Epic Candy Tale.* Diner Mighty Graphics, 2022.

Lager, Fred "Chico." *Ben & Jerry's: The Inside Scoop.* Crown Publishers, Inc., 1994.

Markel, Howard. *The Kelloggs: The Battling Brothers of Battle Creek.* Pantheon Books, 2017.

Rancatore, Gus, and Helen Epstein. *Ice Cream Man: 25 Years at Toscanini's in Cambridge, Massachusetts.* E-book, Plunkett Lake Press, 2019.

Schultz, Eric B. *Weathermakers to the World: The Story of a Company, the Standard of an Industry*. Carrier Corp., 2012.

Shapiro, Laura. *Perfection Salad: Women and Cooking at the Turn of the Century*. Farrar, Straus and Giroux, 1986.

Stone, Orra L. *History of Massachusetts Industries: Their Inception, Growth, and Success*. Vols. 1–4. S.J. Clarke Publishing Co., 1930.

Untermeyer, Louis. *A Century of Candymaking, 1847–1947*. Barta Press, 1947.

Wilton, David. *Word Myths: Debunking Linguistic Urban Legends*. Oxford University Press, 2004.

Cookbooks

Allen, Mrs. Willis H., ed. *Machias Cook Book*. C.O. Furbush, 1899.

Bryan, Mrs. Lettice. *The Kentucky Housewife*. Facsimile ed. Originally published in 1839. Applewood Books.

Farmer, Fannie Merritt. *The Boston Cooking-School Cook Book*. Little, Brown, and Company, 1896.

Howard, Maria Willett. *Lowney's Cook Book*. Revised edition. Walter M. Lowney Co., 1908.

Jones, Judith, and Evan Jones. *The Book of New New England Cookery*. University Press of New England, 2001.

Parloa, Maria. *Miss Parloa's Kitchen Companion: A Guide for All Who Would Be Good Housekeepers.* 19th ed. Estes and Lauriat, 1887.

———. *Miss Parloa's New Cook Book: A Guide to Marketing and Cooking*. Estes and Lauriat, 1880.

Rosenberg, Judy, with Nan Levinson. *The Rosie's Bakery All-Butter, Cream-Filled, Sugar-Packed Baking Book*. Workman Publishing, 2011.

Simmons, Amelia, and American Imprint Collection. *American cookery, or, The art of dressing viands, fish, poultry, and vegetables: and the best modes of making pastes, puffs, pies, tarts, puddings, custards, and preserves: and all kinds of cakes, from the imperial plumb to plain cake, adapted to this country, and all grades of life*. Printed by Hudson & Goodwin for the Author, 1796.

Wakefield, Ruth Graves. *Ruth Wakefield's Toll House Tried and True Recipes*. M. Barrows and Company, Inc., 1940.

Interviews and Correspondence

Fitzpatrick, Meghan. Zoom interview, October 8, 2024.

Gilson, Douglas. Telephone interview, August 11, 2024.

Graney, Mimi. Zoom interview, September 19, 2024.

Green, Jeffrey. Personal interview, March 22, 2024.

Herrell, Judith. Zoom interview, March 7, 2024.

Hintlian, Fred. Zoom interview, November 21, 2024.

Lacey, Darlene. Zoom interview and follow-up email correspondence, August 29, 2024.

Mawhinney, Louise. Personal interview, February 8, 2024.

Myers, Patrick. Zoom interview, February 27, 2024.

Picard, Malaika, and Gerard Picard. Zoom interview, February 17, 2024.

———. Personal interview, July 18, 2024.

Rancatore, Gus. Personal interview, September 30, 2024.

Rosenberg, Judy. Email correspondence, November 21, 2024.

Schober, Meredythe Jones. Telephone interview and email correspondence, October 17, 2024.

Schultz, Eric. Zoom interview, September 6, 2024.

Swantkoski, Sara. Email correspondence, January 29, 2024.

Trieble, Miranda. Zoom interview, March 4, 2024.

Young, Candy Daggett. Telephone interview and email correspondence, October 13–17, 2024.

Selected Articles and Websites

Abelson, Jenn. "Feuding at Friendly's." *Boston Globe*, October 5, 2011. www.bostonglobe.com/business/2007/03/18/feuding-friendly/IB6A4RJwSGo5yq4xI82GCJ/story.html.

Boston Sunday Advertiser. "Daggett Chocolate Co. Has Sweet Success Story." July 27, 1952, 19.

Broekel, Ray. "Ten Immortals." *American Heritage* 37, no. 6 (October–November 1986). www.americanheritage.com/ten-immortals.

Burns, Richard M. "Necco Churns Out the Hearts." *Harvard Crimson*, February 15, 1997. www.thecrimson.com/article/1997/2/15/necco-churns-out-the-hearts-pa.

City Notes, City of West Haven, Connecticut. "Creator of Mounds Candy Bar Cited Posthumously." February 14, 2020. www.cityofwesthaven.com/CivicSend/ViewMessage/message/103975.

Daly, Christopher B. "Boston Suburb Makes a Date to Celebrate the Fig at Cookie Centennial." *Washington Post*, May 4, 1991. www.washingtonpost.com/archive/politics/1991/05/04/boston-suburb-makes-a-date-to-celebrate-the-fig-at-cookie-centennial/9be4523b-b119-4bcb-b615-af5ca448b409.

Fox, Raina E. "Shoelaces and Marshmallow Bunnies: Memory, Adaptation and Reuse at Pawtucket's Hope Webbing Mill." In *Rhode Island History* 74, no. 1 (Winter–Spring 2016).

Gould, John. "As Maine as Lobster." *Christian Science Monitor*, October 24, 1986. www.csmonitor.com/1986/1024/uham.html.

Gully, Andrew. "Vince's Magic Ice Cream Kingdom." *Boston Globe*, June 28, 2016. sponsored.bostonglobe.com/rocklandtrust/vinces-magic-ice-cream-kingdom.

Harrison, J.D. "When We Were Small: Ben & Jerry's." *Washington Post*, May 14, 2014. www.washingtonpost.com/business/on-small-business/when-we-were-small-ben-and-jerrys/2014/05/14/069b6cae-dac4-11e3-8009-71de85b9c527_story.html.

Hurwitz, Mark. "Did You Know: Dr. Laskey and the Ribbon Candy Maker." *Marblehead Reporter, Wicked Local*, December 18, 2020. www.wickedlocal.com/story/marblehead-reporter/2020/12/18/marbleheads-dr-laskey-and-ribbon-candy-maker/3966353001.

Kawash, Samira. "Hershey's: Why a Kiss Is Just a Kiss." *Candy Professor*, March 3, 2010. candyprofessor.wordpress.com/2010/03/03/hersheys-why-a-kiss-is-just-a-kiss.

The Kennedy Center. "Writing Spotlight: 'School House Candy.'" www.kennedy-center.org/education/networks-conferences-and-research/research-and-resources/vsa-research-and-resources/writing-spotlights/school-house-candy.

Marchese, David. "Ben & Jerry's Radical Ice Cream Dreams." *New York Times*, July 27, 2020. www.nytimes.com/interactive/2020/07/27/magazine/ben-jerry-interview.html.

Maynard, Micheline. "Whoopie! Cookie, Pie or Cake, It's Having Its Moment." *New York Times*, March 17, 2009. www.nytimes.com/2009/03/18/dining/18whoop.html.

Muhammad, Khalil Gibran. "The Sugar That Saturates the American Diet Has a Barbaric History as the 'White Gold' That Fueled Slavery." *New York Times*, August 14, 2019. www.nytimes.com/interactive/2019/08/14/magazine/sugar-slave-trade-slavery.html.

Muther, Christopher. "In Memoriam: Boston's Last Surviving Friendly's Has Closed." *Boston Globe*, March 22, 2024. www.bostonglobe.com/2024/03/22/lifestyle/bostons-last-surviving-friendlys-has-closed.

Newspapers.com.

Raposo, Jacqueline. "Colonial America Was Obsessed with Chocolate That Probably Tasted Pretty Bad." Vice.com, January 22, 2019. www.vice.com/en/article/colonial-america-was-obsessed-with-chocolate-that-probably-tasted-pretty-bad.

Rosen, Samuel. "How School House Candy Started." *Rhode Island Jewish Historical Notes* 11, no. 3 (November 1993).

Rotondi, Jessica Pearce. "Why the Candy Bar Market Exploded After World War I." History.com, January 13, 2021. www.history.com/news/wwi-1920s-chocolate-candy-boom.

Schultz, Eric B. "'We Wuz Robbed': A Tale of Innovation, Genealogy, and Taffy-Pulling Machines." *The Occasional CEO*, September 15, 2021. theoccasionalceo.blogspot.com/2021/09/we-wuz-robbed-tale-of-innovation.html.

Severson, Kim. "Sonkers, Grunts, Slumps and Crumbles." *New York Times*, July 1, 2013. www.nytimes.com/2013/07/03/dining/in-search-of-the-sonker-a-sweet-denizen-of-surry-county-nc.html.

Shea, Andrea, and Nora Saks. "Unwrapping the Lost History of Confectioner's Row." WBUR, November 22, 2022. Transcript from *Last Seen* podcast. www.wbur.org/lastseen/2022/11/22/lost-history-confectioners-row.

Tremaine, Julie. "The World's Longest Candy Counter Is in This Tiny New Hampshire Town." *Forbes*, February 26, 2019. www.forbes.com/sites/julietremaine/2019/02/26/the-worlds-longest-candy-counter-is-in-this-tiny-new-hampshire-town.

Tucker, Aimee. "Cobbler vs. Crisp—Funny Names for Old-Fashioned Fruit Desserts." NewEngland.com, August 9, 2022. newengland.com/food/old-fashioned-fruit-desserts.

Videos and Podcasts

"Bite-Size Candy History: The Original Necco Wafers Flavors of 1906." YouTube, uploaded by the Candy Wrapper Museum, June 27, 2022. /youtu.be/kBSa2zuLxnw?si=ebk4Cm21Z_ljNn93.

"5 Secrets of the Jordan Marsh Muffin Man's Recipe." WCVB-TV.

"Flavor Graveyard's Dearly De-Pinted." YouTube, uploaded by Ben & Jerry's, October 7, 2015. youtu.be/qFY6tdbS9Mg?si=ZQg-i5wReePqn3YG.

"Ice Cream Brothers: A Grotto Short Film." *Grotto*, June 26, 2023.

"Legendary Boston Baker Shares Recipe, Techniques for Making Jordan Marsh's Blueberry Muffins." WCVB-TV. April 7, 2016.

"90s Nostalgia: Looking Back at Brighams Ice Cream." *Chronicle*. WCVB-TV, August 18, 2023.

"The Way the Cookie Crumbles." *Gastropod*. Season 17, April 19, 2022.

ABOUT THE AUTHOR

Susan Mara Bregman is an author and photographer living in Boston.

She received a bachelor's degree from Brown University and a master's degree in city and regional planning from the Harvard Kennedy School. After a career in public transportation, working as a public official and private consultant, she has returned to her first love—writing books and taking photographs.

She is the author of *New England Neon*, *New England Candlepin Bowling* and *Along Route 1: Maine, New Hampshire, and Massachusetts*—all for Arcadia Publishing.

She loves roadside attractions, flea markets, lawn flamingos, mahjong and—of course—whoopie pies.

Her photography portfolio is online at www.rednickel.com, and she posts on Instagram and Facebook as @RedNickelNeon.